Endorsements for
eXPlore *Like a Pirate*

"Turn your class into an adventure! This book dispels the myths of games and gamification and shares keys for energizing and exciting a classroom. *Explore Like a Pirate* It's is a must-read for teachers looking to energize and excite their students."

ALICE KEELER, Author of *50 Things You Can Do with Google Classroom*

"Imagine your classroom as an epic adventure where students level up, work together, and learn as they complete grand quests. In *Explore Like a Pirate*, Michael Matera leads teachers on an epic quest to engage, excite, and bring joy back to the classroom through creative gamification and game-based learning. Game-based learning and student engagement is not a myth, make it your reality with this motivating, practical book for teachers everywhere. I highly recommend *Explore Like a Pirate*."

VICKI DAVIS, Teacher, @coolcatteacher Blog, BAM! Radio host of Every Classroom Matters, and Author of *Reinventing Writing*

"Matera takes his years of practical knowledge in using game-based education and anchors it in an entertaining, yet user-friendly, guide that teachers can read today and use tomorrow to get their students having fun while being actively engaged in content. He understands today's learner and provides helpful tips and strategies for teachers to transform their learning environments into one that encourages students to intrinsically take risks, persevere, collaborate, and 'level-up' as they exponentially grow like never before!"

ERIN KLEIN, Teacher, Keynote Speaker, and Author

"Michael is a true pioneer of game-based learning. He understands the power of a game-based approach to both deeply reward and motivate learners, whilst also inspiring the curiosity which empowers them to shape their own destiny and unlock their fullest potential.

"*Explore Like a Pirate* is delivered with the authority you'd expect from someone who has implemented a true game-based approach in his classroom for years. I love the fact Michael is able to show the tangible impact gamification has had on his students over time, whilst sharing strong and passionate arguments against all the skeptics out there!

"*Explore Like a Pirate* inspires a creative and collaborative learning space grounded by powerful pedagogy. Michael explains how it can be adopted by anyone, regardless of experience, subject, ability, age and access to technology. Not only is it the ultimate guide for implementing game-based learning (with examples that can be adopted instantly), you can use this book to sell the strategy to your organization."

JAMIE BROOKER, Co-founder and Chief Creative Officer of Kahoot!

"In *Explore Like a Pirate*, Michael Matera takes the concept of gaming and explains it in terms that could make sense to any educator. He also dispels many myths on why it wouldn't work in the classroom, and gives examples of high-tech, low-tech, and no-tech ways that you can make this happen in your classroom. It is easy to read with actionable ideas you can use in your classroom immediately."

GEORGE COUROS, Speaker, Division Principal, and Author of
The Innovator's Mindset

"*Explore Like a Pirate* allows you to 'level up' the learning in your classroom by exploring actionable ways to introduce or enhance gamification in the classroom. Michael Matera writes from deep experience, having successfully navigated the challenges and practicalities of changing his own classroom. Here, he plots both the why and the how to make learning (and teaching) more engaging and fun in and out of the classroom."

ADAM BELLOW, Founder and President of
eduTecher and eduClipper

"Whether you're an enthusiast or a skeptic about the role of gamification in education, you should dive into Matera's book. His classes have inspired his students year after year, class after class, and *Explore Like a Pirate* helps us understand why."

TED DINTERSMITH, Author of *Most Likely To Succeed*

"Michael Matera is a pioneer in the field of educational gamification and game-based learning. I have great respect for his work, as he has influenced me, as well as other members of my PLN, effectively making him 'my gurus' guru.' Frequently, educators teach in the same ways that we learned. Today's students, however, tend to learn best when exposed to instruction that meets them where they are. Gamification, or 'applying the most motivational techniques of games to non-game settings' is one way to do just that.

"*Explore Like a Pirate* is a must-have tool in the arsenal of the innovative teacher. The book effectively paints a picture of gamification, detailing the many benefits to students, such as allowing them to take ownership of their learning, while cultivating soft skills such as collaboration and empathy. The practice also allows teachers to get to the heart of learning, in building positive relationships with students. The book also presents some examples of game-based learning, which Matera adds as another layer to motivate students. Gamification and/or game-based learning can be used by any educator for any subject and any age group, and this book will tell you exactly how to do it!"

SARAH THOMAS, Speaker and Regional Technology Coordinator

"*Explore Like a Pirate* will empower you to set sail for a new land of learning—one without worksheets and standardized tests. Young or old, all students should be engaged in challenging and immersive learning games: *Explore Like a Pirate* will satisfy that need. Whether you are brand new to the concept of gaming in the classroom or a seasoned sailor on the high seas of classroom games, Mr. Matera's *Explore Like a Pirate* is for you."

JAMES SANDERS, Founder of Breakout EDU

"If you think motivation, engagement, and passion are golden doubloons in the learning treasure chest, Michael's book, *Explore Like a Pirate*, can provide you with a map and compelling directions to help you find your way to the big, black X."

KEVIN HONEYCUTT, International Speaker and Educational Futurist

"Gamification is one of the most important yet easily misunderstood instructional strategies in schools today. In *Explore like a Pirate*, Michael Matera provides an extremely practical, helpful guide for teachers wanting to gamify learning in their classroom. I highly recommend this book. By applying the concepts, strategies and philosophy Michael clearly explains, you can transform learning for your students by providing deeper opportunities for engaged exploration and collaboration.

WESLEY FRYER, Ph.D., Author of *Playing with Media* and *Show What You Know With Media*

"*Explore Like a Pirate* is a fun and practical look at how gamification can be used in the classroom. It presents gamification in a way that is fun and engaging for beginners and experts alike. It offers easy to use tips and ideas to get started with straight away. Highly recommended to anyone who wants to start using gamification in their teaching."

ANDRZEJ MARCZEWSKI, Gamification Expert and Author of *Even Ninja Monkeys Like to Play*

"*Explore Like a Pirate* is an ideal primer for any teacher who wants to embark on the adventure of gamifying their classroom. Matera channels the buccaneer spirit as he provides a map to help teachers successfully navigate the world of gamification. Drawing from years of experience designing and using games in his practice, Matera dispels myths and misconceptions while delivering a wealth of practical information, countless examples and inspirational anecdotes in a playfully irreverent style. *Explore Like a Pirate* celebrates learning as discovery, engagement and play, and is sure to set the motivated educator on the right course to education's New World."

PAUL DARVASI, Teacher and Game Designer

"*Explore Like a Pirate* by Michael Matera is a must-read for any educator considering the possibilities of gamifying their class! The theory behind this powerful text is rooted in the idea that we can make learning fun for students by anchoring it in creative play (aka gamification) that connects to content-based acquisition. Matera helps readers understand that gamification is possible in any classroom because it is all about creativity. The book addresses many of the myths of gamification and offers practical suggestions for making the shift towards gamifying any classroom.

"As an educational leader, this book helped me see the possibilities of gamification and how it could have a positive impact on students, teachers and learning in general. I was hooked when Matera wrote, 'Be bold, be confident, and hold true to your vision. Above all, be playful! Free your spirit by awakening your inner child and you will remember the true joy of discovery. It is the act of discovery that makes playful learning meaningful.' Anything that helps bring joy back into the classroom is worth consideration and implementation. So, the time has come to unleash the creativity in our learning spaces and consider embracing gamification as a way to frame creative learning and empower our students to take control of their learning, which is a victory for all in my book!"

DR. TONY SINANIS, Speaker, Author, and Principal

"Just when I thought we didn't need another book about gamification, Michael Matera graces us with a comprehensive, thought-provoking, and enjoyable guide to how and why to create a game-inspired classroom. He covers all the bases to dispel the myth that gamification is simply about adding badges, achievements and points to an otherwise unchanged class experience. He gets right to the heart of key elements that demonstrate the value of creating a game to immerse our students in the content. I am a huge proponent of student choice as the key element to effectively empower students in their learning. When choice is at the center of a game inspired classroom students take ownership of the learning. Matera speaks to the importance of student choice among other key elements to effective use of a gameful approach. In addition, Matera speaks to the importance of narrative and character development strung through the course in order to truly create a game out of the class experience.

"In addition to touching on all the important elements, the ideas are backed up by research and real examples to demonstrate why this approach is so refreshing and exciting for both the teacher and the students. This book does a fine job of setting the stage and explaining gamification while also providing a clear guide to creating this environment. I have been gamifying my class for years and reading Matera's book got me very excited to iterate on my current model to ensure that I employ the elements that my approach has been missing. Well played, Mr. Matera!"

STEVE ISAACS, Teacher, Video Game Design and Development

eXPlore like a
Pirate

Engage, Enrich, and Elevate Your Learners with Gamification and Game-inspired Course Design

By

Michael Matera

eXPlore like a Pirate

© 2015 by Michael Matera

This book is available at special discounts when purchased in quantity for use as premiums, promotions, fundraising, and educational use. For inquiries and details, contact us: shelley@daveburgessconsulting.com.

Published by Dave Burgess Consulting, Inc.
San Diego, CA
http://daveburgessconsulting.com

Cover Design by Genesis Kohler
Editing and Interior Design by My Writers' Connection

Library of Congress Control Number: 2015956684
Paperback ISBN: 978-0-9861555-0-5
E-book ISBN: 978-0-9861555-1-2

First Printing: November 2015

Contents

Thank you.

A number of people have enriched and made this project possible...

I want to first express my love and gratitude to my partner, Heidi, and daughter, Mila, for their love and support throughout my writing of this book. Heidi, in your hands this book took shape, through late night conversations, careful edits, and the priceless gift of time. As a family, we can accomplish anything, and I look forward to a lifetime of adventures together.

Adam, as my friend and colleague you have challenged me to be the best version of myself. Best of all, you helped me see that we can change the world, one day, one lesson, one tweet at a time.

Any explorer on a voyage is helped by all the fellow travelers and those who pass by along their way. I couldn't have got to this point on my lifelong voyage without my Professional Learning Network. Whether as close colleagues at University School of Milwaukee or virtual partners around the world they all inspired and helped me.

Lastly, the students and their legacies. They made it happen. They stepped away from average and created something extraordinary. The journey, the grind, and the hustle are by no means easy but they put in the time and reached for greatness. This is truly what the New World of education is all about.

Are You a Pirate?

Teaching like a pirate has nothing to do with the dictionary definition of a pirate and everything to do with the spirit. Pirates are daring, adventurous, and willing to set forth into uncharted waters with no guarantee of success. They reject the status quo and refuse to conform to any society that stifles creativity or limits independence. They are explorers who take risks and are willing to travel to the ends of the earth for educational treasure. They yearn for adventure and are constantly searching the horizon for new opportunities.

Teaching like a pirate is, quite simply, a way of looking at the world. Educational pirates relentlessly seek and discover what engages people and then ask, "How can I use that in my classroom?"

There is no denying the enormous pull that gaming has on many youth today. Therefore, the pirate philosophy demands that we examine what makes gaming so engaging and then explore the multitude of ways we can incorporate those elements into our instruction to create enthralling learning experiences for students. This manifesto by Michael Matera on gamification and game-inspired course design is the start of an awesome adventure that may just change your classroom forever.

Best wishes from the captain as you embark and learn to *explore* like a pirate.

DAVE BURGESS
President of Dave Burgess Consulting, Inc.
Author of the *New York Times* bestseller, *Teach Like a PIRATE*
and co-author of *P is for PIRATE*

Join the crew at

ExploreLikeAPirate.com!

Share your questions and

ideas using #XPLAP.

Welcome aboard!

PART I
PLOTTING THE COURSE

*Don't tell people how to do things,
tell them what to do and let them
surprise you with their results.*

—George S. Patton, Jr.

The Call of the Explorer: Discover the Adventure that Awaits

Exploration is really the essence of the human spirit.

—Frank Borman

Are you ready to explore gamification and game-based learning? Are you ready to set sail and transform your classroom into an experiential world that flourishes on collaboration and creativity? I believe you are because, even if you simply picked up this book out of curiosity, you have already experienced the engaging power of creative play.

Now, imagine creative play that is based in content acquisition and student experience. Imagine what it would be like to facilitate an environment where learning knows no borders, no limits, and where maximizing the potential of your students is a reality. Intrigued? Then weigh anchor and hoist the mizzen because together we are going to venture into the seas of gamification. In these first few pages, you will come to realize that this innovative teaching tool is not only possible, but it is also a shipshape way to give life to course content and purpose to students' lives in the classroom and beyond.

In recent years, I have been fortunate enough to travel across the United States to present on the topic of gamification and game-based learning. I have met gifted and passionate innovators who excel at creating and tapping into the very best resources for their classrooms. These bold educators, along with the recent pedagogical tools, are shaping the "New World" of education! As a life-long learner, I am constantly exploring how methods like project-based learning and blended and flipped teaching can enhance my classroom. Professional development opportunities, social networks, cutting-edge research, and daily trial and error help to shape my continually evolving view of the classroom. These explorative channels directed me towards gamification.

Gamification, done with intention, is a perfect vessel to augment many pedagogical tools. It allows teachers, students, and administrators to have what I call an "educational mashup." Gamification and game-based learning have the power to amplify what happens in your class. When created with the meat of rich content, the breath of the current educational movement, and the spirit of collaboration and creativity, you have a fully functional, dynamically successful classroom. However, if done without purpose or personal buy-in, *"shiver me timbers!"* these ideas are easily forgotten skeletons.

Again, whatever your reason for picking up this book, there is something in here for you. As a teacher, I know the importance of making game-based learning tangible in order to get buy-in from students, fellow teachers, administrators, and parents. As you sail through these pages, you will be motivated to think outside the spyglass and see beyond the bounds of traditional teaching methods. You will gain confidence in the many ways gamification already naturally flows with your existing classroom currents. Even if you only venture into a few simple gamification techniques, you will discover ways to maximize your students' potential and their desire to engage in learning.

Administrators and parents, I know what you're thinking because you've told me. This cannot be "real learning," "competition should not be a motivator," and "where is the academic rigor?!" I will address all of these and more.

Finally, gamification provides us the avenue to support the expertise that both teachers and students bring to the classroom. I will share student examples of gamification and feedback from parents who have experienced the wide-open seas of cognitive, personal, and social growth. The best part is that gamification is a collaborative effort that invites opportunities to design and work with colleagues and educators around the globe because gamification has the power to transform the way we teach and the way we learn.

So with that said, where do we begin? We first need the confidence to shove off from the familiar dock.

When first thinking about applying gamification in my classroom, I wasn't sure where sea winds would take me. I was even uncertain if taking time to incorporate gamification was worth the educational benefit. Then I remembered being a kid and how my classes, while

Gamification has the power to transform the way we teach and the way we learn.

interesting at times, were more often unmotivating. Like many kids, I wasn't very inspired by the idea of college (which seemed so far away) or by threats about what would happen if I didn't achieve high letter grades and test scores.

What tipped the scales for me to give gamification a shot was the following childhood memory...

It was just another day in middle school in little old Port Washington. The time was slowly dripping by, and my fellow students and I felt as if we were merely taking up space. I began to daydream. Looking around, I didn't see my classmates; I saw twenty-six secret CIA agents who were uncovering a plot to destroy the world. We were

 **You will see how game-inspired learning creates fantastical experiences that tap into endless reservoirs of imagination and ambition.**

trained and ready with the skills and knowledge to defeat "the enemy." Our teacher was the CIA Captain, charged with giving us the mission to shut down this plot. How awesome! I was transported into a larger world, one where anything was possible, and my classmates and I were at the center of it all!

Looking back on this childhood memory, I understand now that what I longed for was adventure. I wanted to be part of something greater. While my classmates and I wouldn't have articulated it in this way, what we wanted was an immersive experience, one that engaged us on all levels. We wanted a risky mission, in which we could discover the content, come together to overcome conflicts, and make tension-filled choices that would impact "the game" of learning.

As you explore gamified opportunities with your students, you will discover that the power of play in the classroom activates the human spirit and leads to greater content acquisition and self-motivation. Gamification provides an environment that awakens the dormant explorer inside each one of us. You and the students will completely invest in the learning process when your minds, bodies, and spirits are engaged. Instead of being a captive audience, your students will be *captivated* by the adventure of learning. And you will see how game-inspired learning creates fantastical experiences that tap into endless reservoirs of imagination and ambition while also supporting a sense of community through a positive classroom culture.

All the resources you need to gamify your classroom are available within you, your students, and the community of educators you turn to for insights and inspiration. This method is accessible to all grade levels, subject areas, and educational budgets. How? Because you are maximizing what you already have and what is available to you. You start with the content that meets your required standards and then explore how to layer gamification over the top. Game-inspired course design works in tandem with your curriculum standards while offering ways for students to go beyond the basics.

Gamification is possible in any classroom because *creativity* is the wind that powers the sails. Creativity exists inside all of us, even in the toughest buccaneers to bring on board, because we all have interests, passions, and ideas. Creativity is foundational in the New World of education and a tool too powerful to waste. In the pages ahead, we will discover ways students can gain the invaluable life skills of crafting their own educational journeys and taking greater responsibility for their knowledge, behaviors, and motivations. You will learn to create

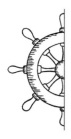

Gamification is possible in any classroom because creativity is the wind that powers the sails.

opportunities for students to explore, practice, and embody skills like confidence, focus, resilience, dependability, curiosity, and empathy while working collaboratively towards a common goal. Part III of this book provides basic game theory and mechanics that will empower you to create an environment that more fully engages students' motivations to learn while also producing better results. We, through gamification and playful planning, will create leaders, critical thinkers, and even legacy makers.

Oceanographer Don Walsh described exploration as "curiosity put into action."[1] Be a curious, ambitious explorer as you embark upon the journey of this book. Allow the ideas to transport you outside your comfort zone and to see new possibilities in what you are already doing. You may take away a few gold nuggets or perhaps a treasure chest of ideas to hone your skills and expand your resources. I encourage you to forge ahead even if, like the early explorers, you have no idea what awaits you. You may be approaching this with a mixture of skepticism, fear, and excitement; and yet you are here on the dock because you also dream of what could be possible when teaching and learning are action based and inclusive of the individual skills that everyone can contribute.

So take the leap and come aboard. The best explorers were those who had the drive to understand things that others couldn't even imagine possible. You know the content; now let's infuse game-based strategies that will unlock your students' potential and shape their futures.

RESOURCES

1. Andrew Howley, "2012 Explorer of the Year and Hubbard Medal Winners," *National Geographic Society*, June 15, 2015, http://voices. nationalgeographic.com.

Tall Tales:
Dispelling the Myths
of Gamification

*Understanding is the sum
of misunderstandings.*

—*Haruki Murakami*

Still have a toe on the dock? Perhaps misconceptions about gamification are keeping you from jumping aboard. This chapter will quell your fears by answering common questions and concerns about game-based learning. What you'll learn here will also help you convince administrators, parents, students, and colleagues—your crew—that this is a journey worth exploring. Get their buy-in and you'll be one step closer to setting sail.

So, let's start with the most common question I hear: *What is gamification?*

Gamification is applying the most motivational techniques of games to non-game settings, like classrooms. This simple definition is a great place to begin the conversation, but there is so much more to this pedagogical tool. Gamification includes elements of game theory, design thinking, and informational literacy. It is a framework laid over your curriculum that is fluid and tangible at all skill levels.

Success comes when we are intentional about the ways we use gamification in tandem with curriculum standards. What we are essentially doing is an educational mashup of game-based learning, plus other tried and true methods. Sailing forward, remember we are using gamification to enhance what we already do.

Identifying and overcoming the misconceptions about gamification helps ensure a positive gamified experience for students, parents, and administrators. Let's learn from the myths, avoid them, dispel them, and especially not perpetuate them. The proof will be identifiable when you start seeing positive results from the beginning.

MYTH #1
Games are just for play.
There is no challenge or educational rigor.

TRUTH
Games are filled with a motivational complexity that can be used to shed light on topics and increase content acquisition.

Serious games, sometimes referred to as *applied games*, fall into a category of strategic play with purpose beyond pure entertainment. Do a simple Internet search, and you will discover that professionals use games to solve real-world problems in industries like federal defense, education, scientific exploration, healthcare, emergency management, city planning, engineering, and politics. Learning by doing, commonly referred to as *experiential learning*, is a powerful tool many educators already use. Through games, we allow students to learn from mistakes, practice both short- and long-term planning, and, best of all, develop informational literacy skills. Informational literacy is the ability to select the best option in an ever-changing environment—a challenging but valuable life skill!

Have you ever sat down and played a video game with your nephew or niece or some other member of generation G, the gamer generation, and found yourself with two left thumbs while they are succeeding right and left? This isn't luck; it is a skill that can be transferred to our

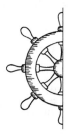 **Bringing the positive, result-producing aspects of games to the classroom is key to the intentional use of gamification.**

classrooms and in daily life. Today's games are far more complex and demanding than the Pong of the past. They require kids to multitask and handle multiple inputs at any given moment. Games are rigorous, and they elicit the honing of vital skills, such as critical thinking, intuition, and communication.

Bringing the positive, result-producing aspects of games to the classroom is key to the intentional use of gamification. The goal is to design a series of challenges that students will find worth exploring. In that exploration, their learning goes well beyond the basics. Just like choice games do—the games students choose to play at home—we can strategically make our game components more challenging so that kids will stay engaged. In doing so, we create a classroom environment that fosters the students' desire to learn—because learning feels like play.

So let's investigate why students play choice games like video games and board games. No one makes them play; they do it on their own and in their free time. As the gamer generation, their number one use of time is to play games. They game more than TV, movies, and trips to the mall combined. By the time our students complete high school, they will have gamed for more than 10,000 hours[1]. As educators, we need to meet our learners where they are, and they are gamers!

Let's stop for a moment and think about what this $300 video game machine really is. It is a little box that produces very difficult challenges and tasks to solve. Honestly, doesn't that seem like the worst birthday gift for your thirteen-year-old? *Hey, I bought you the best gift ever... I bought you a workbox. Yeah, right!*

Let's compare the workbox to the class workbook. The video game machine (workbox) and the class workbook are very similar when stripped down to the basic components. Both have points, levels, cheats, and allow players to develop over time through completing tasks or challenges. Yet the class workbook is often uninspiring and demotivating. Why? One reason is that workbooks don't allow for choice. Game systems, on the other hand, incorporate choice and motivational mechanics, such as questing, gaining access, and preserving the open-ended process by giving agency over to the player. When we follow suit and structure these elements into our content, student motivation and knowledge acquisition increase. Building course work through the eyes of a game designer will provide you with the insight necessary to create a New World of learning.

In the old world of education, choice games and our classes have little connection in students' minds. I have discovered several reasons for this. As teachers, we have been trained to provide little challenge. We are taught to model, model, and then model some more. By the time the students get to create, they feel little motivation to do so. That ship has sailed, usually more than once, and they want to move on to the next task. We also show them "behind the curtain" too early in the acquisition process by giving them rubrics that spell out each and every detail they will need to address to succeed. What I have experienced is that overuse of rubrics encourages students to create "inside the box" projects, instead of tapping into their creativity that goes beyond what any rubric would measure. In my classroom, I want students to create and perform from a place of passion and drive because that's when they are motivated to tackle the challenges of the content and assignments. Their learning then takes hold in a greater way, which produces better results on assessments and in students' overall acquisition.

So, how can you enliven your content and course? Start doing what I call *playful planning*. Literally, take your content and play with it; think of ways to make it accessible to students that are "outside" the normal box of worksheets, lecturers, reading materials, movie hour, etc. Then, engage your students on a whole new level by allowing them to play with the content by infusing some of the game mechanics within your course. Giving students opportunities to have direct control over the game will result in players and students who feel connected and inspired to dive deep into the content. When you do an activity that is slightly out of the norm, the students, not knowing what to expect, will be more vigilant and eager to participate, which only adds to the excitement of the task. Harness the open-ended, non-scripted aspect of games and give the students the autonomy to take a project where their interests lead.

Challenging your students engages them and creates a positive force for learning. It's about finding the flow. Game designers know that players walk away from games that are either too easy or hard. Finding that "sweet spot" for the gamer is what psychologist Mihaly Csikszentmihalyi calls *flow* found in *Flow and the Foundations of Positive Psychology*. Flow is a state of heightened focus and immersion one experiences while participating in activities such as art, play, and work. Mihaly has devoted his life to the study of what makes people truly happy and has discovered that *flow* is where the magic of happiness and optimal performance meet. He defines flow as the creative moment when a person is completely involved in an activity for its own sake. He says, "When we are involved in [creativity], we feel that we are living more fully than during the rest of life."[2] By using gamification, we can incorporate the power of flow into our classrooms and encourage self-motivation and "happiness of doing" in our students.

According to Psychologist Mihaly Csikszentmihalyi, people feel best when they are at the perfect level of their skills: neither under-challenged (boredom) nor over-challenged (anxiety and frustration). And, as people learn with time and repetition, challenges have to increase to keep up with growing skills.

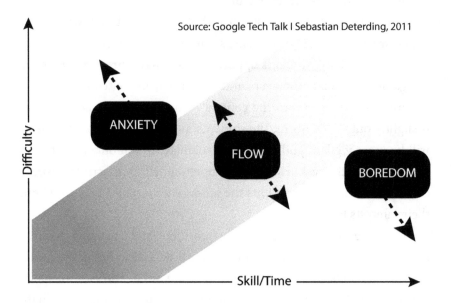

Source: Google Tech Talk I Sebastian Deterding, 2011

Teachers who only focus on the rigor and not the flow prevent their students from achieving their full potential; rigor without flow is just hard for hard's sake. Grounding our intention in Csikszentmihalyi's ideas, we can produce the right results for our gamified classroom by fusing together the ideal amount of content, choice, and challenge.

The three Cs of content, choice, and challenge are important to keep in mind as we design the elements for game-based learning. *Content* is the curriculum and required standards. *Choice*, in the open-ended game model, is an invitation for students to explore unique, individual paths to content acquisition. *Challenges* are the unknown twists and turns that keep the learner engaged throughout the unit. Allowing for content, choice, and challenge to merge in a way that puts the student in control is no easy task, and that is where an intentional gamified structure is essential. You can structure a system that encourages kids to explore, tackle what lies ahead, and, as Csikszentmihalyi's studies show, do it all with smiles on their faces.

MYTH #2
If I give them a badge or points, my class will be gamified.

TRUTH
Combining the many elements of game mechanics helps create memorable experiences that push students well beyond the bounds of the traditional classroom.

When I first started looking into the topic of gamification a few years back, the only tools I could find were badges and points. Badges and points, without an engaging setting or purpose, were not motivators for me or my students.

Monopoly is a good example of an engaging game with purpose. After each round, you earn points and badges in the form of money and properties. These rewards are exciting because there are other elements at play. First, there is meaningful social interaction between the players inside the overarching storyline or theme of the game. Second, there are the micro-goals, like free parking, getting a set of properties, and building a real estate empire. Third, there are the risks and challenges that result from your choices. All of those elements combined make it something that kids and adults can play for hours. If the game were simply about collecting points, Monopoly wouldn't be one of the world's best-selling games; in fact, it would be boring. The same is true for our classrooms.

You will learn in the pages ahead that points and badges are only two of the many game mechanics that support gamified lessons, units, and courses. A healthy gamified classroom must include a variety of elements that build upon one another and create opportunities for effective communication and collaboration among students.

MYTH #3
It's easy for you. It won't work for me because I teach _____ [Fill in the Blank].

TRUTH
Gamification works for all grade levels, subject areas, and educational budgets.

This myth is just plain bunk! I understand that you might not want to change your class, or you have concerns about the time needed to make a change. But saying you can't gamify your class because of the subject you teach is simply an excuse. Gamification is possible in any subject because it's not as much about the content as it is about engaging students in the learning process. Gamification is successful in pre-kindergarten classrooms all the way up to advanced placement and international baccalaureate classes because it connects content with the way students act and think. The question shouldn't be *if* you can connect it to your content; it should be *how* you are going to connect to your students. Take your subject, lay over the top of it a gamified structure that motivates students, and you will start to see the true power of this educational tool. Remember, this method is available to you no matter what grade, subject, or diverse student body you teach. Yes, it will take time to create. It will force you to think differently about your class. But one thing that it won't be is unavailable to your class due to your course topic.

MYTH #4
You need to be a gamer
to gamify your class.

TRUTH
You do not have to be
a gamer to get started.

An explorer is an explorer once she sets off on the voyage of discovery. Likewise, you will be a gamer once you start to gamify your classroom. You will find how accessible this method is when you invest the time to learn simple game designs and mechanics while letting your creative winds blow. You will continue to be motivated to build your newfound game knowledge because you are creating a learning experience that is both unique and memorable.

Start building your ship ledger by doing a bit of fun research. Download the latest or most popular game apps and start playing them. Note what aspects engage you as possible elements to include in your classroom. Take note of the overall game structure and specific goals and challenges. After doing this research, your legal pad or digital document will be filled with random musings that will provide a motivating starting point for your game design. Part III of this book will provide you with additional ways to begin brainstorming ideas as well as guided processes to structure your gamified lesson, unit, or course.

MYTH #5
Students should want to learn;
I shouldn't have to dress it up!

TRUTH
Finding meaning in our content
unlocks students' motivation.

I agree and disagree with this misconception. Yes, students have all sorts of responsibilities, and, truth be told, they are not always fun. But, students' lack of attention or desire should not be the only argument that teachers make regarding students who are currently disengaged from the class. We knew when we became educators that we would be tasked with finding meaning in our content and keys that unlock students' motivation to learn it. Intentional game design provides an environment that allows the students to "dress up" their learning process in a way that both motivates and produces achievement results.

Teachers want to unlock students' potential and push them to do their very best. Gamification does this by building meaningful experiences within the content. Those experiences are then amplified through the individual ways students choose to engage with the content. Adding gaming elements to lessons should not be seen as a move away from rigorous education, but instead, as a move into real-world problem solving, project-based learning, and design thinking. By focusing on the game of the lesson or unit, you support students' exploration of personal skills and interests that they may not yet be aware they possess. Students will gain new skill sets, tackle difficult challenges, and ultimately become lifelong explorers, discovering both the answers they seek along with their passions.

MYTH #6
Gamification is just playing games...

TRUTH
Gamification is more about exploration of the course, content, and your crew than it is about playing a game.

When you gamify your classroom, you take the best, most motivational aspects of games and apply them to your course content. Gamification is a tool you can use to motivate, inspire, and take kids on an adventure within the course content. Through game mechanics and game elements laid over the top of your course, you will increase students' motivation, passions, and willingness to explore the learning opportunities.

Truthfully, this myth is the most commonly believed. Almost every time I talk with people about the topic of gamification, the first thing they bring up is how much they like the game of Monopoly and that they should include more games in their classroom. Monopoly is a natural connection and one that often links fondly to childhood. It conjures up warm memories of playing on the living room floor and driving a hard bargain with siblings. The second bridge many make is that gamification is only about board games and how to use them in the classroom. Although I love seeing them make those mental connections between games, fun, and learning, I patiently wait for the opportunity to expand those connections. I will never argue with the positives of a solid board game, but it isn't what gamification is about. My desire is to help people understand the real magic of gamification. I want to help educators learn from the gaming industry and embed the most motivational aspects of games into what they are already doing in their classrooms.

Once people start to talk about what gamification really is, there is a shift in the conversation. What started with warm and fuzzy childhood memories turns into resistance toward a practice they don't have time for in their classrooms and finally evolves into the understanding that creating the necessary changes and incorporating gaming adventures in learning is well worth their time and effort. When they begin to understand that gamification pairs easily with what they are already doing and acts as a spark to fuel students, they get excited about its potential.

MYTH #7
Girls don't game.

TRUTH
Girls not only game,
they dominate the game world.

Take a look at who is playing games:
- In 2014, 52 percent of the gaming community was comprised of girls.[3]
- 38 percent of players are women over the age of 18, compared to 17 percent boys under the age of 18.[4]

Simply put, *girls are gamers!* They love to achieve, they have drive and determination, and they enjoy playing games just as much as the boys in your class. In my gamified classroom, the top players every year are a mix of boys and girls. Gamification doesn't favor one gender over the other. By using the tool of gamification, we are able to get the best out of all our students.

MYTH #8
My classroom doesn't have enough technology to make this work.

TRUTH
Gamification can be high tech, low tech, or no tech.

By now I am sure you understand that we aren't talking about playing full-production games in the classroom. We are overlaying our course content with aspects of games—challenge, mastery, story, and choice—that motivate and inspire our students toward action. You are the game master. You can create the kind of game you want. You can use web tools, online leaderboards, and badge-infused learning management systems. Or you could easily have a bulletin board for a leader board, printed badges, and game mechanics that use very few resources.

Don't let the absence (or fear of) technology scare you away from this wonderful tool. While there are tech tools that I use in my classroom, I would never say they are required. In fact, in the ten years that I've been incorporating game elements in my classroom, I've often discovered that the best games require no technology. Success of gaming has a great deal to do with socialization, which is *free* and something our students are exposed to every day.

MYTH #9
Games in the classroom are
too much about competition.

TRUTH
Positive competition can inspire collaboration
and motivate students to do their very best.

Your colleagues and administrators may struggle with this misconception because of the negative pitfalls often associated with competition in the classroom. And yet, we know competition on the court or on the field brings scholarships and recognition. Positive aspects do exist in competition, and game-based learning has the potential to support the positive motivation needed to achieve one's fullest potential.

In my own classroom, the benefits of healthy competition became obvious during a yearlong gamified course. My students had to learn to work effectively in teams to overcome challenges and unlock mysteries to accomplish the content goals. What they internalized was not the competition but the skills required to collaborate and achieve the desired outcome. Together, these students shared purpose and a clear vision of what was necessary to succeed.

THE EARTH IS NOT FLAT—
AND YOU ARE NOT ALONE!

Now that we've addressed and dispelled the fears and myths surrounding gamification, we can begin preparations for exploring its vast possibilities. Remember that as an educational explorer, you are not alone. You are part of a community of educators, gamers, and designers that will support your vision, help you avoid the pitfalls of these myths, and navigate the challenging conversations. Hold on to your newfound confidence as we push off for the New World.

Resources

1. Gabe Zichermann, "How Games Make Kids Smarter,"
   TEDxKids@Brussels, June 2011, https://www.ted.com/talks/
   gabe_zichermann_how_games_make_kids_smarter.

2. Mihaly Csikszentmihalyi, "Flow: The Secret to Happiness," *TED*, October 2008,
   https://www.ted.com/talks/mihaly_csikszentmihalyi_on_flow.

3. Meg Jayanth, "52% of Gamers Are Women—but the
   Industry Doesn't Know It," *The Guardian,* September 18,
   2014, http://www.theguardian.com/commentisfree/2014/
   sep/18/52-percent-people-playing-games-women-industry-doesnt-know.

4. Gail Sullivan, "Study: More women than Teenage Boys Are
   Gamers," *The Washington Post,* August 22, 2014, http://www.
   washingtonpost.com/news/morning-mix/wp/2014/08/22/
   adult-women-gamers-outnumber-teenage-boys/.

New World, Old World

*Man cannot discover new
oceans unless he has the courage
to lose sight of the shore.*

—Andre Gide

As an educational explorer, you have creative confidence to forge out into the unknown. Trust in the process, and believe in yourself. We are about to apply your passions at a deeper level in your classroom.

My passion for gamification stems from a belief that, like the early explorers, we must continually discover methods to move away from the unbending, monolithic structures of education. The educational structures built on the needs and desires of our great grandparents' generation are fundamentally different from those of students today. And yet, many schools are still practicing two-hundred-year-old traditions. We must adjust our thinking to align with the new movement in education. The New World in education requires us to look past the old ways and create more dynamic learning environments and methods of teaching. This New World will most certainly incorporate parts of the old world; however, we need to look beyond what we do in order to create, see, and even understand a new reality.

Old World	New World
Traditional, fossilized ways of teaching	New and innovative ways to connect and inspire students.
Controlling	Freedom & flexibility
Produces followers	Produces risk takers
Plotted path	Sense of exploration and discovery
Quiet compliance	Creative confidence
Automatons of knowledge	Independent artistic thinkers
Constructing lessons	Creating heroes
Passive receivers of content	Sense of wanderlust, spirit, and passion

Gamification is one of many new and innovative methods that moves us from the old world into the New World. It provides the structure needed to move beyond the regurgitation of memorized content. It allows teachers to create challenging and motivating experiences that meet *and* go beyond the required curriculum standards, while captivating students' minds and feeding their hunger for knowledge. Game designers stand by the notion of "that which is earned is learned." Students want a personalized experience and a sense of autonomy. Mihaly Csikszentmihalyi explains, "It seems increasingly clear that the chief impediments to learning are not cognitive in nature. It is not that students cannot learn; it is that they do not wish to."[1]

GAMES MAKE KIDS WANT TO LEARN

As educators, inspiring self-motivated learning is the key. We as teachers need to embrace the organic nature of learning. The focus on standards, common core, and district initiatives, while important, are not what touches the souls of our students. We are not teaching standards, we are teaching students—children who have passions, questions, and the drive to make a difference. As teachers, we have the honor of fostering their creative confidence and compassionately daring them to reach for their dreams. By helping them tap into the joy of discovery, we equip them to use a powerful tool that is essential to solving the world's challenges today. When we inspire students to go beyond what they know and to venture into the unknown, we change the future forever.

In my gamified class, students see themselves as key players in their own learning. To them, school is as much about developing their skills, by attempting quests that expand their horizons, as it is about learning the content. The game model provides feedback loops, which encourage students to actively work towards becoming the best versions of themselves, and different game mechanics reach different students in various ways. You'll be amazed as you watch your students overcome challenging obstacles with enthusiasm and self-motivation.

Inspire the Extraordinary

Throughout the year, my students learn several mantras from me, the first of which is, "Strive to do the extraordinary." We live in extraordinary times with access to extraordinary tools. Why not do something extraordinary?!

I also tell them, "Life is about choices, so choose wisely." I encourage them to invest time in activities that stretch their skills, push them to try new things, and explore the world. My supportive challenge for you is to connect with your students at the gut level. Be adventurous, and choose to try new techniques that will help you build an experience that will last well beyond your class.

I teach a world history course, so it only makes sense that another mantra in my class is, "Life is all about leaving a legacy." I talk with my students about ancient civilizations and the legacies that defined them, like the Pyramids in Giza and the Great Wall of China. I ask my students what their legacy will be and how they will be remembered. Since most kids aren't great at thinking about their long-term

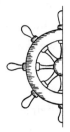

The power of play brings back the natural yearning that exists inside all of us to learn.

legacy (few of us actually are), we don't talk about the distant future; I ask them how they will be remembered *today*. I want my students to understand that each day is a new opportunity to shape their futures and that life doesn't start in college—it begins now. Most of all, I want them to be captains of their own destinies and rise above the great waves of mediocrity.

Since using gamification, I have seen an upsurge of the extraordinary among my students. Parents call me to say they have never seen their child so engaged in a subject, let alone history. They seem shocked, but it makes sense to me. You see, the human spirit awakens when we are inspired and challenged to confidently go beyond our limits. The power of play brings back the natural yearning that exists inside all of us to learn. Students are motivated by the challenge, enthralled by the discovery, and proud of the accomplishments that last well beyond the school year. Additionally, gamification requires students to be part of a team, so they end up pushing one another to be extraordinary. When you are as committed to your students' individual needs as you are their learning, you will find or create the means to provide an even richer environment, knowing their lives will be forever shaped by their experiences.

FLEXIBLE AND FUN

One of the things I love most about a gamified lesson or unit is the ability to change it. Since they are already familiar with the multiple worlds or levels in a game setting, they are open to changes within the course. This is fantastic for me because, as a teacher, I thrive on being responsive. It gives me the flexibility to put into practice what I learn at conferences, edcamps, and Twitter chats. I no longer have to wait for the coming year to try new things. Instead, I get right down to business with the best pedagogy and newest technology tools of the New World in education. As you sail with me over the next few chapters, you too will find the freedom within this unlimited method of teaching and learning.

An Example of the Extraordinary

One legacy I will never forget happened at the beginning of the school year. As part of the Egypt unit, I offer an optional *Da Vinci Code*-inspired hunt with clues scattered throughout the school. The storyline was that Imhotep, the architect of the pyramids, had gone missing. He must be located in order for the pyramids to continue construction; without him, their glory will never come to pass. Remember, this was not a required activity but a quest that they would have to tackle in their free time.

As word spread, so did interest in the quest. Students began by reading the backstory about how Imhotep went missing and then encouraged one another to take on the challenge of finding him. I added to their motivation by announcing that Pharaoh's riches would be given to any team that finds him. As part of accepting the mission, they had to ask me for Imhotep's last scroll before he went missing. Inserting myself into this part of the quest allowed me to keep track of who was participating.

Once a few students got their scrolls, others started asking questions. "Hey, what's that all about?" "It looks fun!" or, my favorite, "That sounds like a lot of work. You guys are going to need me on your team. Can I join you?" Soon after the first group formed and started working on the riddles during study hall, about 75 percent of the students were trying to find Imhotep. The race was on!

I designed this scavenger hunt to take almost the entire unit to figure out. I intentionally made it hard enough so that some groups would give up and, in fact, many did. In the end, I had only three teams reach the final clue. Because some groups gave up their hunt to find Imhotep, the remaining groups pushed even harder and experienced a greater sense of accomplishment when they found him. These students created Google Docs to share notes about the clues and riddles. They searched rooms, the Internet, and read books to find the answers. Through each step of the way, their confidence grew in themselves, their team, and their knowledge of history. They loved the hunt, and they formed strong bonds as members of a team, which still last to this day.

Resources

1. Mihaly Csikszentmihalyi, *Creating for the Future*, (New Horizons for Learning, 2002) John Hopkins School of Education. http://education.jhu.edu/PD/ newhorizons/future/creating_the_future/index.cfm.

Part II
Scallywags and Seadogs

*In your life, you choose and create
the people and events designed to
bring you the perfect opportunity to
know yourself as you truly are.*

—Neale Donald Walsch

All great explorers were visionaries, risk takers, and determined adventurers. However, they were never alone. These men and women, who explored the far reaches of both the world and the mind, were part of a crew. From Christopher Columbus to Madame Curie, these explorers all needed others to believe, help, and in some cases follow them—no matter the adventure.

As you set out on your gamification exploration, remember you are not alone. Colleagues, students, parents, administrators, and your personal learning network are on this journey with you. In fact, these people are stakeholders in your expedition. They will offer valuable advice from their own perspectives. While these people offer their help, suggestions, and fears about the possible pitfalls for what lies ahead, remember *you* are the explorer—the leader of this adventure. Be bold, be confident, and hold true to your vision. Above all, be playful! Free your spirit by awakening your inner child, and you will remember the

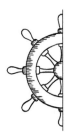 That moment, the leap from the mechanical to the organic, is what I want to recreate for my students.

true joy of discovery. It is the act of discovery that makes playful learning meaningful. As developmental psychologist and philosopher Jean Piaget said: "When you teach a child something, you forever take away his chance of discovering it for himself."

We are all born knowing how to play. When my young daughter Mila learns the rules for a game, she is very focused. She begins by playing the rules mechanically, until she starts to discover new strategies. That moment, the leap from the mechanical to the organic, is what I want to recreate for my students. I don't want them to be limited by the constraints of rubrics and standards all the time. I want them to find the freedom to play and explore within the content.

In game-based learning, we must give our learners structure by teaching the content and defining the rules of play. That framework gives them the ability to make choices, which lead to greater discoveries about their own learning. Mila, like my students, naturally asks questions about the rules and the strategic options as the game progresses. This allows her to form her own intuitions about the game, which hopefully lead to victory.

This section is aimed at providing the tools to better understand your crew—your scallywags and seadogs. As the teacher and new game designer, you will learn exciting ways to motivate, inspire, and engage your students. You will master a new language of learning that leads your students to become educational explorers. The tools you'll discover are those that enable me to help my students get the most out of the classroom, while also teaching them about themselves. Some of the tools came from game designers, while other tools are from teachers. It is my hope that they will help you better understand your students.

Ahoy Mate!
A New Language of Learning

*A different language is
a different vision of life.*

—*Federico Fellini*

When I first started to gamify my course, my goal was engagement. I wanted students to be excited, and I wanted learning to be playful again. I soon realized that games tapped into something far greater than mere engagement. This style of teaching inspired students. The more I gamified my course, the more I saw a need to change the language of learning. Layering the game over my entire course encouraged collaboration and offered a ton of self-exploration. Learning was no longer about earning a grade; it was about discovery and growth. One of my former students sums it up best:

Before I came to Mr. Matera's class, school and classes were just something I showed up for to get grades. But that all changed this year. Mr. Matera is no ordinary teacher; he got everyone excited about school. The gamification that Mr. Matera created made students more excited about class than anything else. I saw my best friends, who used to care nothing about school, spending hours a week working on an extra credit project or, as we called it, a "side quest." Friends uncovered hidden talents and discovered new interests. But the thing that made gamification so great was the fact that the students in our grade learned more than we ever would by just studying the textbooks. His class helped us develop skills and passions that we will have the rest of our lives. I speak for my whole grade when I say that Mr. Matera changed the way we learn and inspired us to do more in and out of the classroom. Mr. Matera made my classmates and me want to come to school.

PURPOSE-DRIVEN LEARNING

Getting students to view education this way didn't happen overnight. It took time and an intentionally different way of talking about learning. I was fortunate to learn about this new language through a fellow teacher and friend, Adam Moreno. The idea was simple—he came up with ten words that gave students the tools to be successful, not only in school but in life. He identified a list of ten qualities highly successful people have in common—confidence, creativity, enthusiasm, effort, focus, resilience, initiative, curiosity, dependability, and empathy—and then used these words to define and drive what he calls Purpose-Driven Learning.

These ten words have forever changed the way I talk with students, and they continue to be at the core of my gamified classroom because they lead students to take personal responsibility for their learning. Purpose-Driven Learning has become a common language for me and my students that we use to define and discuss the classroom norms and goals. Likewise, they serve as a foundation for what it means to effectively work and succeed together as we embark on a shared journey of self-discovery. History is the study of the greats—great leaders, great moments, and great change. Having a language built on action-oriented words helps my students carve their own paths toward becoming the best versions of themselves.

Whatever the language you want to use, it's important to remain consistent. A poster of the Purpose-Driven Learning words hangs in my classroom as a reminder that this is our language, our system of measurement for being the best version of ourselves. I use them daily in class discussions, in report card comments, when talking with parents, and when explaining an upcoming project. With Purpose-Driven Learning as our primary language, thoughtful discussions about the power of curiosity and resilience, focus, effort, enthusiasm, and confidence replace conversations about grades. Encouraged to think about their own growth goals, students now take the action needed to improve their results—and learning.

Since Purpose-Driven Learning has changed the way students talk about their learning, I no longer hear typical sixth-grade responses, like "I need to study more" or "I should work harder." They now understand these are hollow and nebulous goals. Instead, they talk about their own need to take the initiative in exploring what the course has to offer, or to have greater confidence in order to embrace a growth mindset, or to be curious enough to discover their passions. I am thrilled with the powerful change that has happened in my classroom through the combination of gamification and Purpose-Driven Learning.

Since this is a new way of speaking about learning, I find it helpful to bring parents on board from the beginning. I begin each year by sending home a letter that introduces both gamification and Purpose-Driven Learning. Feel free to use or adapt this letter to help introduce the concept in your school community.

Hello Parents,

I want to welcome you to the adventure of sixth grade world history. This year your children will not simply be taught the content; they will experience the learning. Through my years of teaching, I have developed a system around the concepts of Purpose-Driven Learning and gamification.

Purpose-Driven Learning is the backbone of my classroom. The purpose of school is not simply to get good grades. The purpose needs to be learning and helping the children become life-long learners. These qualities can be encouraged at home as well as in the classroom. By utilizing the keys of Purpose-Driven Learning, we can help the students understand the qualities needed to be successful in any classroom and in the world beyond school.

Gamification is the idea of applying the most motivational aspects of games to other industries, like education. For example, in a game, children are willing to try over and over again, simply to make it to the next level. I have found that gaming concepts, like intrinsic motivation, self-taught exploration, and learning through failure, have transferred to the classroom with great success. However, a key part of this success is that the learning is student driven.

Learning to take the initiative in their schoolwork, attacking each assignment with enthusiasm, creativity, and effort, and overcoming challenges with their own curiosity and resilience builds independent learners. With parents' support of the gamification system and the encouragement of their child's ability to put the keys of Purpose-Driven Learning into action, we can work as a team to help these young learners reach their full potential.

My class is designed to be challenging. They will be asked to complete work that will require them to explore and seek out the answers. At times, they will find great success. Other times, they will experience failure. As adults, we understand that in the struggle is where the learning takes place.

Ultimately, your children are the players of this game we call school. Does it engage them? Does it challenge them? Does it encourage them to explore, fail, and try again until they succeed? It is up to the students to seek out knowledge and demonstrate resilience to overcome obstacles this year. Learning in this type of environment is a proven way for students to become life-long independent learners. Please allow your child to explore the wonders of history, make mistakes on their own, and learn from the journey.

Let the games begin…

When I first introduce gamification to parents at back-to-school night, they seem intrigued and bewildered. By the time parent-teacher conferences roll around mid-term, the bewilderment is replaced by excitement. The conversations change from questions about "why gamification?" to "where else will my child experience this powerful teaching style in school?" Most of my students' parents tell me they have never seen their child have such drive and enjoyment at school. They tell me they have never seen their child work so hard and have such passion for learning. Once a parent described that their child now has a "fire in their belly." Another parent told me, "This was my son's favorite class. I have never seen him so motivated to go beyond the basic expectations. Phenomenal idea of having 'side quests' to motivate. This should be the model for all educators!" Another parent wrote me a note that read, "I have never seen my son so excited and interested in learning! He routinely (with no nudging!) went out of his way to research, do side quests, and go beyond the expectations, purely because he was enjoying the process and learning. That is the mark of true excellence—when you can spark a student to not only learn what is expected but also to be engaged enough to have the initiative and curiosity to explore beyond the expectations and discover their true capabilities."

Critics of gamification question how to measure these *Kum-Ba-Yah* moments in the classroom, but isn't this what we want for our own children? In my experience, parents want their kids to learn, laugh, and love their way through their education. I have found that game-inspired course design is the best way to create that experience and achieve meaningful and powerful results. These words that define Purpose-Driven Learning have opened up new conversations with and possibilities for my students. Let's explore a few ways they can be used in your classroom.

CONFIDENCE

As a small child, one's hopes and dreams are endless. Young children truly believe they can achieve anything as long as they try. In kindergarten, kids learn through play, they *experience* learning; questions drive their classrooms, rather than just the facts. As educators, we must remember that it was exploration, not memorization, that expanded the worlds of early learners and mapmakers alike. As students get older, encouraging them to take risks and giving them the space to explore our content helps them grow in confidence. Not every attempt will result in a success; however, students will gain greater confidence when allowed to explore. I tell my kids that learning is like climbing a mountain; there are many paths to the peak. Although it can be tricky, it is well worth an educator's investment to identify those paths that ensure students both acquire the necessary knowledge and have the freedom to express themselves in thoughtful and creative ways.

I often talk with my students about owning their decisions. I see how students feel paralyzed by the fear of being wrong. The creative freedom that once flourished in their hearts now lies dormant. The truth is that the educational system has created this lack of confidence

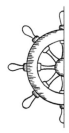 We must remember that it was exploration, not memorization, that expanded the worlds of early learners and mapmakers alike.

with its command-and-control environments. Students are given rubrics and study guides. They sit through mini-lessons and endless modeling. All this hand-holding creates a passive and paralyzed student body. If we want to end this cycle, we are the ones who need to change.

At first, your students will be challenged by (and maybe even afraid of) their newfound freedom. They have become used to the mechanical nature of school. Here is where their lack of confidence will become apparent. They may not know where to start and even *request* the rubric. But rubrics are recipes, and we must stop creating cooks who follow recipes. We must begin inspiring students to, like chefs, confidently create their learning experiences.

CREATIVITY

Since the information age now fits into our pockets, content is no longer king. Content is now virtually free and streams to our smartphones, smart watches, and tablets, wherever we are. Wikipedia, the world's free and open-source encyclopedia, has displaced an entire industry. Massive open online courses, or MOOCs, are changing the way people pursue higher education. Success no longer comes from what you know; it is the result of what you do with what you know.

The future belongs to those who can apply knowledge in new and innovative ways. That means that helping our students strengthen their creative muscles is time well spent. Don't be afraid to allow for creative freedom and construct risk-rich environments. Assign open-ended tasks and resist the urge to spell out every detail. Using game-inspired course design will encourage your students to shift their thinking from content to innovation and, at the same time, will result in better understanding of the content and stronger, more prepared, and more creative students.

ENTHUSIASM

Have you ever watched a good comedy by yourself? It isn't the same as when you are together with friends, and even strangers, in a theater. In a group, the laughter and joy spreads and changes the entire experience. Enthusiasm is infectious.

I regularly tell my students that I want them to bring enthusiasm to class. When several of my students show up ready and determined, the entire feel of the class changes. The other students can't help but get pumped up.

Enthusiasm in the classroom is a two-part job. First, as educators, we have to create experiences that are worth getting excited about. Because, let's be honest, while it is easy to show enthusiasm for the things you love, being enthusiastic about tasks you dread is hard! Second, we need to remind students to be open-minded and enthusiastic towards even the most challenging, less-engaging tasks—for the benefit of their classmates as well as themselves. It takes time, but students learn the lesson that Zig Ziglar taught us: "Your attitude determines your altitude."

EFFORT

Education is like any endeavor: you get out of it what you put into it. Hard work is a stone and effort the chisel. Teaching students to chip away at the stone day in and day out will help them reach their full potential. If we want our students to achieve greatness and leave a legacy, then we must help them understand that putting forth their best effort every single day is a must. Beyond succeeding in the classroom, effort is important to every area of life, which makes this attribute one of the most important we can instill in our students. Continue to have conversations with your students about how and why to apply themselves. Within my class, the side quests are great spaces to show off creativity, initiative, and effort. When students take the simple, open-ended directions of my quests and fully apply themselves to the task, we are all blown away.

FOCUS

Focus is a key skill that can be difficult to master at any age. In my own classroom of middle school students who tend to want to run off in just about every direction, focus requires intention and practice. Focus is used when entering a class discussion, reading their homework, and interpreting directions. It is also needed when completing tasks. Students need to learn to keep focused on many moving parts during a speech, a group task, or an after-school performance. I've found that my students need to be reminded of this skill all the time. Some are great in class and are able to focus intently on the discussion but then drop the ball when reading directions. Other students struggle with background noise within the class. No matter what the reason for the distraction, learning to control one's thoughts is essential. Guilds are a great way to increase students' focus on excellence in all areas, without you becoming each student's personal focus master.

I talk about the power of the guild to support, as well as push, one another to be their best. By limiting myself to encouraging the guilds and leaving the details to the guild members, students start to improve their ability to focus on the details because they want to have strong members of their guild.

RESILIENCE

We need to help students understand that they learn as much, if not more, from their failures as they do their successes. Teaching students that the word *fail* really stands for First Attempt In Learning is a great first step. Helping kids understand that learning is a process, we provide them with a chance to be explorers and encourage them to attempt to set S.A.I.L. (Second Attempt In Learning). From a student's perspective, if a teacher says fail is just a "first attempt" but still applies a failing grade based on that attempt, the student has "lost." But if students expect that second and third attempts inevitably follow first attempts, and the grade isn't dependent on that first attempt, then the student feels more confident knowing he or she has a chance at success. The student will then be less likely to give up before learning the material. Gamification encourages students to do their very best

We need to help students
understand that they learn as much,
if not more, from their failures
as they do their successes.

the first go around, and if they don't succeed, they may attempt the challenge again. I love the focus on personalized mastery that is built into gamification. This teaching format allows students to fail, redo, and reach mastery in many different ways.

Resilience is more than just perseverance. Perseverance is about hard work and strong effort, while resilience is about adapting and overcoming obstacles. Throughout their education, students will encounter many obstacles. If we can foster a comfort level around resilience and second (and third, fourth, and fifth) attempts, the focus becomes the goal—learning—rather than just the grade.

INITIATIVE

Initiative is a skill students master through game-based learning. Right from the start, students instantly understand that taking initiative is the way to go if they want to win. Initiative comes in all shapes and sizes. For example, I offer optional side quests that encourage students to challenge themselves and dive deeper into the content. By

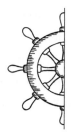

Inspire students to rise above mediocrity and do the extraordinary.

showing initiative and going on these quests, students find greater success within the game and the course. But even for those who choose not to participate in the side quests, my class requires going above and beyond, which inspires students to rise above mediocrity and creates students who, without prompting, take it upon themselves to do the extraordinary. Over the year, they develop into creative, independent learners. They learn how to seek out answers to their questions, solve problems, and overcome challenges—all without help. By making initiative a habit in my students' lives, they discover just how capable they truly are.

CURIOSITY

Sparking curiosity sets the mind on fire. If we can connect our students' passions to our content, we will ignite their drive to learn. Every course offers the potential for wonder and *aha* moments. And as the Socratic Method teaches us, answers come with even more questions. Teaching students to be okay with this endless cycle of *listen, process, ask, and repeat* will empower them with confidence to explore. They'll experience the joy that comes with being curious about our content and, more importantly, life beyond the school walls. Our job is to encourage them to embrace (or rediscover) their natural curiosity and then follow their questions to find answers—and even better questions.

Learning, in the most authentic sense, is curiosity. It begins with a question, a need, a want, a desire to understand something. From there, we embark on a quest to understand our question. We search for answers anywhere we can find them. Play toward your students' curiosity. Drop hints of things to come, start a rumor about an upcoming team challenge, and be playful by allowing students to imagine what is to come in your course or game. If you want a big bang in your class, use anticipation. It is curiosity's fuel.

DEPENDABILITY

No great explorer sets out alone. Each of them depends on others for help along the way. Their faithful crew members are their friends, loyal comrades, and loved ones. Explorers in the classroom need the benefit of a crew as well. By providing opportunities for authentic collaboration, we can help students understand and appreciate the interconnected nature of our classrooms. When students come prepared for class, a high level of cross-pollination can take place. Ideas can be discussed, shared, and built upon. Students gain trust in one another as they start to see just how much they have to learn from one another.

In my gamified class, students are part of a team. Their class is a house, and their group is a guild. Both of these communities provide opportunities for them to work with and help one another. The more they work together and get to know and draw upon one another's strengths, the better they do. In this environment, students learn just how dependent we are on one another. Through the year's many collaborative endeavors, students experience what it feels like to be an integral part of a team. They develop a sense of real belonging, something that is often missing in schools when the only focus is students' individual letter grades.

EMPATHY

All of the attributes that comprise Purpose-Driven Learning require empathy. Students need to give and receive empathy on their journey through K-12 education. We need to teach students how to be more inclusive, how to respond to other students' questions, and how to build healthy relationships with one another. Take the time to establish with your students that your classroom is a safe environment to express oneself, take risks, and learn from failure. Set ground rules that encourage them to respect one another's opinions, even if they disagree. Helping your kids feel both safe and invited to share their ideas allows them to come out of their shells ready to learn. When students are able to connect on a personal, more empathic, level with their classmates, they can take the personal risks needed to grow and learn.

These are the keys of Purpose-Driven Learning. This is the language that I speak in my classroom because it allows me to talk to students about their growth. Through the years, conversations shifted from just making a grade to leaving a legacy. These conversations put the focus back on learning. These qualities help students focus on powerful paths towards success. As I started to gamify my course, I noticed that I was doing far more than teaching my students; I was helping them discover the joy of learning. With the rise of creative work that my students were producing on these quests, Purpose-Driven Learning gave me a voice with which to lead and inspire my students. I learned that if we want to inspire kids to go above and beyond, we as teachers need to change the language of school. I tell my students every year

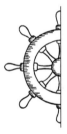

Good teachers build relationships on connections not corrections.

that I am their academic coach. I am here, helping them reach their goals. As they produce passion-filled, artistic wonders for these quests, I can't just grade them. Students don't just want a number, they want a connection. What they create is now part of them; it is their artistry manifested for all to see. So don't just give a grade, or even a badge; you need to listen and hear about the process they went through. Comment on the struggle, discuss the brilliance, and thank them for the courage to tackle these quests on their own. When a student rushes through a quest and it isn't their best, talk them through their process. Remind them that the initiative to do this quest was only the first step. Greatness requires great focus and effort. To gain confidence on this quest, you need to give yourself the time required to produce the level of work that I know you are capable of creating. Of course, you have the opportunity to tackle this quest again, testing your resilience, and demanding you flex your creative muscle.

Good teachers build relationships on connections not corrections. Take the time needed to get to know your crew. Once you create a real connection with them, you can explore any corner of the world. Like any other change in school, Purpose-Driven Learning will only become powerful if you believe in it. I try very hard to live up to and work toward these words in my own life. I help students realize that they must believe in themselves, be confident in their choices, and strive to be their best in life through purpose-driven learning.

From the Helm:
Getting to Know Your Crew

Alone we can do so little;
together we can do so much.

—Helen Keller

The captain's awareness of his or her crew is crucial to the success of any expedition. Every voyage tests a crew's strength, and understanding each member's shortcomings and talents can make all the difference. A good captain knows when to push the crew members and when to lead them along.

In this chapter, we'll review a few tools that will help you practice game-inspired course design with your students in mind. These tools, developed to help appeal to gamers, have proven to be windows into understanding how to construct course content activities to best motivate and engage students in the classroom.

Player Type Theory

Richard Bartle, the author and designer of the player type theory, identifies four key groups of gamer personalities: Achievers, Socializers, Explorers, and Killers (griefers).

Bartle's theory, which was specifically designed for MMOs, or Massive Multiplayer Online games, offers insight into gamers' likes, dislikes, and motivations. If you think about it, our classrooms fit the first two of the MMO letters and sometimes the third. Schools are massive and multiplayer, and we are constantly moving more toward online learning.

In my own class, I have had students take the Bartle Test at the beginning of the year and report their scores to me. It's just another kind of personality-type activity; however, I've found that understanding my students' reasons for playing also provides insight into how they learn. Below is Bartle's theory of the four different player types and the motivations behind them. (See Figure 1.)

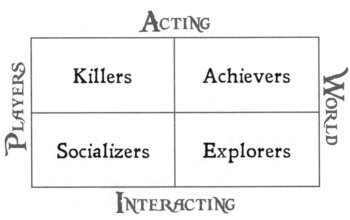

FIGURE 1

This simple graph does a really good job of showing what motivates and feels good to a gamer in an MMO. For example, a *Socializer* connects to *interacting* and *players*. This shows you, without a doubt, what socializers value most. They want meaningful interactions and the ability to connect socially with others in the game.

While we are not creating an MMO, we are looking at applying game design to course design. Understanding your students/players helps you to create game-inspired courses that engage them. For example, each time I create projects and team challenges, I make sure to include something for all the gamer types. Doing so ensures your game really takes off.

A QUICK SUMMARY OF GAMER TYPES

ACHIEVERS

Achievers are the players who strive to gain points, levels, and game items that can be measured against other players of the game to show a level of mastery. They will go to great lengths to earn a reward that offers little benefit to them other than the prestige of the achievement.

In your class, Achievers want to know they are doing well. They will like the status that the game confers on them within the social environment of school. Make the class data public, but don't just think *leaderboard* here. Use small, daily competitions, awarding items, or anything else that shows their position or advancement to stir excitement and drive within the Achiever.

SOCIALIZERS

Many players consider themselves Socializers in the MMO world. These are people who play games for the social aspect of gameplay rather than the actual game because they derive most of their enjoyment from their interactions with other players. The game becomes a tool Socializers use to create meaningful memories and relationships with others.

As teachers, it's easy to associate the term "Socializers" with "talk-ers." But as talkers or "socializers," these players can act as the glue to any group or even your game. Socializers need to have a space to inter-act with others in your class because they are also looking for mean-ingful relationships to be formed during the game. As you design the elements of your game, look for ways to look for ways to create that space and foster positive social interaction. A good place to start might be a team challenge that involves some out-of-class networking oppor-tunities. Certain mechanics, like trading, will appeal to Socializers. The trading mechanic gives them an opportunity to wheel and deal with other players. Another way to encourage interaction among players lies in how you structure your quests. For example, you could design some quests that require players to form a mixed group to go on the quest. This mechanic allows them to use their networking abilities to connect with other players. As a teacher, I make sure I know who my Socializers are. They provide insights into how a group is doing.

EXPLORERS

Explorer is the gamer type I personally identify with the most. Explorers like to dig around in a game. They prefer discovering areas, creating maps, and learning about hidden spaces. They enjoy an open game that allows them to move at their own pace and explore the world. Explorers will try most aspects of your game, but they don't concern themselves with mastery. They will take great joy in discover-ing a hidden Easter egg or a glitch in the game itself.

Within your class, Explorers will not be as vocal about your game at first. Leave that to your Achievers and Killers. In fact, these players will appear to be on the fence about the game. But trust me, they aren't. They are starting the exploration phase by listening to the explana-tion of the game structure. Before you know it, you will have Explorers handing in side quests and looking to find hidden elements within the game. They do great work and are motivated to discover. Have fun designing for the Explorers. Just like the Achiever, the Explorer loves it when others can benefit from their knowledge. Other elements you could add to motivate and inspire are locked areas or levels. They will want to see what is beyond that door and will strive to catch that glimpse, especially if not everyone will get to see it.

Killers (Griefers)

As the name alludes, Killers like to sow destruction in high-action game environments. Killers are also sometimes called Griefers or Conquerors (terms that are more appropriate, perhaps, for school environments). These players enjoy playing the bad guy and are very good at evaluating the cost-benefit of attacking. For example, whereas an Achiever or Socializer might work for seven or eight hours to discover a special sword, the Griefer knows he or she can gain that sword in five minutes by engaging and beating you in a battle. This player is good at quickly assessing the odds of victory. And if the potential reward is worth the risk, game on! Griefers also like to play games in which they have a hand in building or destroying a virtual society.

These players can be very good to have in your game. Their love of competition will add a bunch of enthusiasm to your game. They will be some of your early adopters. Building in game components that appeal to Griefers is pretty easy: they want the ability to grow in power and to be able to use that power in strategic ways. Within my game, students who identify with this player type love collecting items and using them in rumbles against other groups. The flip side is also true. These gamers will be the best protectors of a guild or house. They will be the first to talk about ways to protect and defend what their group has done. Get to know who your Griefers are early on and recruit them to use those skills to protect their house.

Elements of
Game-Inspired Course Design

Jon Radoff is an American entrepreneur, game designer, and the author of *Game On: Energizing Your Business with Social Media Games*. His method for design focuses on four key components that align well with Bartle's gamer profiles. Radoff's four main areas are: immersion, cooperation, achievement, and competition.

Radoff notes that games are experiences and states that "experiences are more about happiness than they are about things."[1] He then challenges designers—and us as educators— to "craft experiences because this is what reshapes your relationship with people." One of the things I love about Radoff's model is how the social (tapping into the human desire to find and create community) and cognitive (engaging our propensity for ideas, language, and stories) aspects of his game design model easily map to the education space.

QUALITATIVE

	FEW PLAYERS		MANY PLAYERS
	Immersion	Cooperation	
	Achievement	Competition	

QUANTITATIVE

Breaking down Radoff's four categories will help you think about different ways to view the elements in your course and inspire you to design new types of activities to deliver course objectives. Looking at the chart above, think about the four quadrants and ask yourself, "Have my students experienced any of these lately?"

Immersion

Immersion is all about storytelling and designing a world that students can relate to and that allows them to explore, grow, and create. In our gamified classroom, we need to look at the larger theme, as well as setting and activities, in order to maximize the immersion experience. Students feel empowered when they are allowed to become the heroes of their own stories.

Achievement

This category is about mastery, giving the player the opportunity to learn and practice a skill. We want to encourage repeat trials to reach the level of proficiency without being punitive during the process. Giving students feedback through various game mechanics can be a great way to show achievement as well as to support students making informed decisions about the game and their learning. The difficult challenge in gamification is finding the sweet spot between making something trivially easy or insanely difficult. Schools are already set up with an achievement structure. Unfortunately, Achievers are the only ones who find that structure motivating, which leaves 75 percent of the student body disengaged. Gamified course design provides the means to engage *all* of your students.

Cooperation

Teamwork is at the core of this game element. Cooperation includes traits like altruism, coordination, coalition building, and grouping or banding together, which appeals to both Socializers and

Explorers. Education is ripe for gamification of this sort. We can create meaningful experiences for our students by encouraging them to build collaborative teams. As team members work together toward a common goal, students develop a solid understanding of the course content and the value of positive communication.

COMPETITION

Competition allows for players to interact with one another, a draw for social players; however, competition is also a powerful draw for your Griefers and Achievers. Competition can be a great way to bond as a group and give rise to a more authentic collaboration. Think of your school's sports teams. Players bond over a highly competitive experience and, at the same time, work to help one another. Competition allows us to build in quantitative tasks and social interaction between groups and students that incorporate important life skills.

SAPS Model

Gabe Zichermann is the author of several books on the topic of gamification, most recently *The Gamification Revolution*. He is the creator and brains behind the GSummit, where leaders gather to learn about the power of leveraging game mechanics to increase user engagement in business, education, and other non-entertainment industries. He also developed the SAPS Model, which I use throughout my course design. SAPS stands for Status, Access, Power, and Stuff. This model is a powerful tool that can help educators to further understand what motivates their students.

The SAPS Model helps me incorporate different motivating factors to create a game-based course that ensures options for all students. I highlight examples of SAPS in Part III when detailing game mechanics. Before we get there, let's take a quick look at each piece of the SAPS Model.

STATUS

As teachers, we have gotten into a habit of stomping out all displays of status in the classroom. We want everyone to feel like a winner. While I understand this intention, I have seen how students stretch (and surprise!) themselves when they are publically recognized for going beyond the basics. Our students need constructive feedback; they also need for us to hold up examples of excellence. Using status as a game mechanic reflects what happens in real life by providing a model of what is truly great and inspiring students toward action. I have seen students' work quality increase dramatically since introducing status into my own course. I believe some of this improvement is the result of the engaging game environment. But I also strongly believe that public acknowledgment of good work has incentivized students to do their best. Shielding students from status limits the learning opportunities by not addressing their need for acknowledgment.

I incorporate status throughout my course by using leaderboards and badges. Knowledge of status supports students to set micro-goals and allows them to see growth of their character through the course. How might you integrate different types of competition in your class? Could you offer new kinds of quests that are outside the norm of your course? Remember: students become motivated when the spotlight shines on them as well as on others.

ACCESS

People love to feel as if they're part of something special, particularly when that access is based on conditions or accomplishments. This innate desire is one of the true powers of game-inspired course design. Engagement increases when students gain access to experiences they didn't have before, including different game levels and secret areas that need to be earned or discovered. Get creative and connect tasks and challenges to your theme. As long as your students are engaged with the required content and course objectives, it is okay if not every student experiences all aspects of your game. Motivation for access is what will take your students well beyond the required content acquisition!

POWER

All game players want some bit of power over the game. Another good way to look at the word power in this context is *agency*. Students, as players, want to be able to make decisions and gain strengths and abilities, which lead to new opportunities and actions.

Of course, you can also literally give students power over aspects of the course. I occasionally do this by giving students choice over their projects or makeup of their work group. You will want to consider the value and the rarity of the power for students. Scarcity is one of the best ways to make something desirable.

STUFF

Physical, non-game-related *stuff* is the least motivational for the engagement of students. Ironically, it is most often used. Think pizza parties, candy, or badges that aren't related to a game. The difference is that game items—a small sword, powerful shield, or disruptor beam— have no real market value, only game value, which keeps the gameplay intrinsically motivating. Done well, game stuff adds to the transformational experience that engages and escalates students toward becoming the best versions of themselves through exploration of the game. While there is a collection of game-related points, badges, and items, they are there only to add to the experience.

All good teachers know the importance of understanding their students. It helps us decide how to handle just about any situation. Moving forward with game-inspired course design, I hope these lenses help you create experiences that are unique and engaging as you reach different types of learners.

When you start your voyage to the New World, remember to include your crew. You will need them on this adventure; you and the students will be the ones who inhabit this New World. As the captain, you must inspire them to explore with you. Show them the value of taking risks and exploring their interests.

Resources

1. Jon Radoff, "Designing for User Motivation," (GSummit, New York, NY, September 2011).

Part III
Setting Sail

Thought is the wind,
knowledge the sail,
and mankind the vessel.

—Augustus Hare

The time has come, matey, to leave the dock and set sail on the high seas of gamification towards the New World of education. Take the plunge, even if you still have doubts and even if you don't yet trust that the risks are worth leaving your safe and settled shores. Think of the treasures of experiences and life lessons that are possible when students are allowed to dream, to create, to flounder, to rise above mediocrity, and to build upon the knowledge and skills they have yet to discover in one another—and themselves. Embrace your inner explorer. Use the pages ahead to expand the horizon of your course content because you are the one who can ignite your students' passion for learning and inspire them to leave legacies.

This section will serve as the key to your map of exploration in gamification. The coming pages are dripping with the tangible concepts and tools you need to gamify a lesson, a unit, or even your entire

> **Think of the treasures of experiences and life lessons that are possible when students are allowed to dream, to create, to flounder, to rise above mediocrity, and to build upon the knowledge and skills they have yet to discover in one another—and themselves.**

course. Together, we will walk through each concept's or element's focused preparation process, something I call Adjusting Your Sails. You'll learn how to catch the wind of focused preparation and discover the right length and pace for your gamified experience. Knowing if it is going to be a two-week unit versus a yearlong game drastically changes how you will go about structuring the experience. You will have to create a much longer arch of success, as well as develop a richer game environment for students to explore, if you build your game to be a yearlong experience.

In the Unpacking the Cargo segments for each concept, we'll review the valuable game elements, such as mechanics, tools, items, badges, and mini-games, which will turn your current content into an even more engaged learning environment. And we won't stop there. Your sea-weathered hands will soon hold the actual designs for gamifying your course.

The Navigating the Waters section is your hands-on guide for story building, setting the course, and exploring routes of possibilities through guided questions and playful planning. Within Navigating the Waters, you will see that the options are endless and routes can be repeated and revisited throughout your design process and beyond.

In these limitless waters, you will decide the creative process that works best for you. You will find your gamification muse from which current and future playful planning will flow. What will spark your desire to press on through unchartered waters? When you find out, you will come back to Part III again and again for reference and fresh ideas for your journey of gamification. The information here will prepare you, sustain you, and lead you beyond your wildest dreams of learning potential for you and your students. Let's shove off; the New World awaits!

A Whale of a Tale:
Theme and Story Telling

*Learning is the human activity
which least needs manipulation by
others. Most learning is not the
result of instruction. It is rather the
result of unhampered participation
in a meaningful setting.*

—Ivan Illich

ADJUSTING YOUR SAILS

The time has come to create our stories and let the winds of imagination propel our voyage of gamification. On this journey, you'll need the heart of an explorer and the confidence of a pirate as you hoist the mainsail of theme and design the setting, characters, and action. We will embrace the freedoms within playful planning and put no anchors on the possibilities that take shape as we explore the plethora of resources around us.

Societies pass down their history in the form of stories. A great storyteller paints a picture in our minds, as well as in our hearts. Shared stories pass on traditions, values, and beliefs from one generation to the next. More than that, they inspire and motivate us toward action. As teachers, we want students to learn how to tell their own stories. In my classroom, we define this as leaving a legacy.

UNPACKING THE CARGO: THEME, SETTING, CHARACTERS, AND ACTION

THEME

Choosing a theme is the first step in gamification and will set the tone for the lesson, unit, or even the year ahead. Theme is the frame of your story, and it provides the backdrop for activities, items, badges, and challenges. You can create a theme around an existing unit or provide an alternative environment separate from your primary content delivery.

Here are a few theme ideas to get you started:

SPACE

FUTURISTIC

FANTASY

EARTH BLOWN UP

STEAMPUNK

HACKER

HIGH SEAS ADVENTURE

EXPLORER

LOCAL, CONNECTED STORY

SUPER HEROES

PANDEMIC

DYSTOPIAN

UNDERWATER

HISTORICAL EVENT, E.G., OLYMPICS, CIVIL WAR, SIGNING OF THE CONSTITUTION

You can also borrow theme ideas from popular books, television shows, or movies. Whether you take the entire theme of *Hunger Games* or just an element from within it, like the kids being from different districts, familiar stories are a great resource. Start with an idea and build on it.

Tisha Richmond, a high school culinary arts teacher, chose the movie *Hundred-Foot Journey* to inspire her story creation. The movie is about restaurateurs who are seeking their next Michelin star. Tisha's class is divided into teams, and each team is a restaurant seeking rave reviews from critics. The goal is to get write-ups in famous papers and magazines around the world, and the main objective is to earn a Michelin star. Once she had the theme in place, Tisha was able to easily design her gamified class.

The theme truly sets the stage for all the other components of your gamified class experience.

SETTING

The theme of your story is a big picture view as vast as the ocean. In contrast, the setting describes the rickety ship and the tossing waves.

The setting is where all parts of the story come together and the players get specific details about the world. Setting is one part location and two parts description as we create a world that awakens the imagination. The setting provides the backdrop for the action and tension in the story.

For example, if the theme is based around the events of a town in the Old West, the setting is so much more than the "old mining town." Setting creates the tangible elements from your theme by helping your students understand the layout and picture the details: the swinging door of the saloon, the corner store's broken window, and the tumbleweed rolling down the empty main street. It is these specifics that make a theme come to life. We must paint the picture for our students; we must verbally create this universe.

A fun place to start is re-theming aspects of your class around your setting. The bathroom pass soon becomes the outhouse pass. A trip to the water fountain becomes a drink at the watering hole. Have students go to the general store instead of the supply closet to pick up what is needed for their next adventure. This will begin setting the stage for a different way of learning because these simple changes tap into the vast sea of creativity that exists in our students' minds. My five-year-old daughter, Mila, teaches me that anything is possible when you're playing. Our minds become untethered through play, allowing us to discover new solutions and answer the impossible questions. The power of play moves us away from average by helping our dreams become our realities.

Characters

The setting you create cannot be a ghost town; it must have characters. Your students will have their roles, while other characters will belong to the game and add to the plots and challenges of your story. Characters drive the game. They are what your students become—the heroes they cheer on and the villains from which they run.

As I developed the elements of the game for my course, the Realm of Nobles, I had to make character choices relevant to my story. First, the king. In my story, he is dead, and now there exists a power struggle throughout the Realm for the throne. The next character I created wasn't a person; it was a people. I made each of my classes a house. Throughout the year, the backstory for these houses unfolds. I talk about the houses, use their names at lunch, and build a lore around them, all of which help the students truly become part of the family within their house.

I have developed other characters, like Edgar the traveling salesman. Edgar appears in each unit as a holder of a secret that students can try to find. If they do, they are allowed to trade with Edgar. He adds familiarity when we travel from setting to setting and helps the story have continuity. The Persians are an example of another character I use to drive my story. During the Greek unit, our final assessment is the last battle between the Persians and the Greeks. This kind of reappearing character has a unifying effect in a game. Players of all houses, just like the Greek city-states, have to band together in order to defeat this enemy. Characters can come in all shapes and sizes. Create characters that will help you achieve the goals you have for your students and you.

ACTION

Lastly, every good story needs some action or conflict. We should build challenges and obstacles that individual students, small groups or bands, and large classes need to overcome; together, they can create an army.

Challenges and obstacles happen on two different timelines. First, we need small, quick challenges that help our adventures feel successful. There must also be opportunities to learn from failures and to make adjustments in order to reach the larger unit or course goal toward which everyone is striving.

In this gamified story model, our content aligns with the students' acquisition of it. As heroes of the story, they become part of the game and create action within the game's theme and setting.

Using all of these elements—theme, setting, characters, and action—and being intentional about your story will allow you to cre-

You will see how gameplay is an explosive cognitive dance that fully awakens the mind.

ate a fully immersive experience for your students. I don't gamify my class every day. However, every day my students exist within the story. As the teacher, you will start the story off by bringing it to life. Don't just wear a cowboy hat on the first day and leave the rest of your course untouched. Take time to integrate the elements of the story into your game-inspired course design.

Once you create a world that transports your students to another way of engaging with the content, you will see how gameplay is an explosive cognitive dance that fully awakens the mind. By gamifying your content, you are building upon the foundation of standards and anticipated grades—not ignoring them. When your students are engaged and excited about being part of the learning adventure, they will meet and even exceed curriculum standards. As the action and conflict taps into their emotions, you'll see their aspirations unleashed. And, as their captain, you'll be there to guide them in directing the course of those newfound aspirations, so they can reach their fullest potential.

NAVIGATING THE WATERS: STORY

It is time to brainstorm ideas for the story of your game. As you navigate the waters, we need to set the course for our final destination. Along the route, you'll want to make sure to explore the details around you. As the saying goes, it is not about the destination, it is about the journey. As you begin the journey of creating your game, it is exciting and fun to think about the endless possibilities. The details of your story make a huge difference in your students' engagement and excitement.

Take some time to answer the questions below. They are designed to stimulate the creative process of clarifying your theme.

Remember—your story encapsulates four key elements: theme, setting, character, and action. Starting with a picture might help inspire creative ideas.

SETTING THE COURSE

Pick a route and answer the question(s). Then move to the next section, "Exploring," and further define the details. Start with the route that excites you the most and then come back to the others later.

ROUTE ONE: THEME

Look back at the list of example themes. Which appeals to you? Which do you know the most about? Find possible themes from books, media, historical events, and your content.

ROUTE TWO: SETTING

Within your themes, what worlds, lands, or environments could exist?

ROUTE THREE: CHARACTER

What general types of characters occupy the world you have created? Who are your students going to be in this world? What characters will come in to help or hinder your students' progress?

ROUTE FOUR: ACTION

What is the main conflict your students are striving to overcome? What are the objectives that your students need to complete? What adventure are they on?

Exploring

Now that you have chosen a route, it is time to craft the details. Use the general ideas you created above, spend time exploring possible names, characteristics, and connections. If you get stuck or lose motivation, move on to a new route and come back later with fresh eyes.

Explore Route One: Theme

Based on your theme, what are the realities that exist?

Examples

- Futuristic: time travel and advanced technologies

- Western: lawlessness and shootouts

- What part of your content fits this theme really well?

- What aspects of this theme will excite your students?

Explore Route Two: Setting

You have brainstormed lands, worlds, and environments within your theme. What are more specific terrains, locations, and buildings within your theme?

Examples

- Futuristic: dome biosphere, high-tech medical clinic, communication headquarters, transporter

- Western: ghost town, desert, cattle drive, saloon

What are the benefits and challenges of these settings for your story? For your content? For your students?

- What are some activities your students can do in these settings? How can these activities tie into your content? On a stranded island, for example, they could go to the beach or go fishing and earn randomly selected bonus points from the "pool."
- Are there creative ways you can incorporate different settings with your theme? e.g., time travel, space exploration, magic, deep sea world.
- What ways can we make your setting a more immersive experience? Are there props or decorations that could enhance the environment for your students?

EXPLORE ROUTE THREE: CHARACTER

What types of characters did you develop when "setting the course"?

- Individuals (mad scientist, king)
- Groups/Families/Guilds or Houses (The Royalty, the Exploration Team)
- Communities/People (peasants, natives)
- Establishments (the church, the government)

Specifically address these questions for each character:

- Where/when will this character be used?
- Is this character a hero, a villain, or a combination of both?
- Is this a main character or a supporting character? Onetime or recurring?
- What is this character's backstory? How does this backstory fit into the larger story?
- What are his or her strengths and weaknesses?
- How does this character connect or interact with other characters you've created?

Explore Route Four: Action

- What are "problems" that arise in your classroom that can be integrated into your story? (Talking out of turn becomes static that blocks important messages from Command.)

- What types of conflicts could exist in the theme of your story? For example, futuristic conflicts might include lack of resources, getting lost during exploration, encountering aggressive alien race. Conflicts in a Western story might involve homesteaders taming the land, a rattlesnake bite, or a shootout.

- What are routine tasks that your students need to complete in order to be successful in your classroom? (vocabulary words, note-taking, test review)

- Connect your theme to the tasks that you listed above. What are creative missions/tasks the characters of your story can undertake? (e.g., vocabulary words = code breaking; note-taking = data mining; test review = mission training)

- What are non-required skills that add to the overall learning of your students? (e.g., experimenting with technology, using artistic talents, exploring a topic of interest in more depth)

- Think of collaborative group work. What types of tasks can your students complete in small groups? As a class? As a grade level? (e.g., groups of four build LEGO representations of content; each class creates its own flag; everyone in tenth-grade advanced algebra works to solve the "impossible" equation faster than last year's students)

Pulleys, Ropes, and Rigging: Game Mechanics to Outfit Any Journey

If you get stuck, draw with a different pen. Change your tools; it may free your thinking.

—Paul Arden

ADJUSTING YOUR SAILS

We have left the docks, raised the mainsail, and now it is time to let out the spinnaker. The spinnaker sail fills like a balloon to propel a downwind course. Some spinnakers are optimized for a particular range of wind angles, allowing captains to maximize each moment. Like the spinnaker sail, this chapter will provide the mechanics for structuring the intricacies of your game. These mechanics work together to build a custom experience that, when combined, lead to memorable moments in your class.

Unpacking the Cargo: Mechanics

It's time to unpack provisions that will feed our creativity and fuel us toward the ultimate goal of building an engaging settlement in that New World of learning. The cargo of this section includes many of the mechanics used in gamification. Many can even be found in full-production games. Victor Manrique's Game Mechanics Tool Kit was instrumental in teaching game mechanics for video game designers. Within this section, we will build upon Manrique's tool kit by learning how to adapt those mechanics for our classroom. Be prepared that not every student will be motivated by every game mechanic. As we saw with the Player Types and SAPS Model, individuals are motivated in different ways. Your goal as a good game designer is to provide a rich game world that includes something for everyone.

Disclaimer: Don't jump ship out of fear now! The following mechanics section is extensive with the purpose of giving you the full breadth of options. Consider it a treasure chest—one to explore in its entirety or to pick and choose from as your game unfolds. Likely, your gamified course will use only two to three mechanics in the beginning. You will come back to this section multiple times during your playful planning. Go to page 134 for the Navigating the Waters guide to mechanics.

Experience Points (XP)

Explanation

An Experience Point, usually shortened to XP, is a unit of measurement used in many role-playing games (RPGs) to quantify a player's progression through the game. These are generally awarded for the completion of game-related tasks, such as overcoming obstacles or defeating opponents.

Players begin the game with little to no XP and, as such, start off weak and untrained. As they earn more XP, they begin to gain powerful upgrades and level up, which are other game mechanics.

Pros

- XP can be a great way to include status in your game.
- This mechanic is found in many games so your students will be familiar with this idea.
- This mechanic is really good to use with other mechanics such as levels, power ups and leaderboards.

Cons

- They are totally worthless if your game system does not use other game mechanics.
- As a stand-alone, points are nothing!

Uses and Ideas

Experience Points (XP) can be a wonderful addition to any game and an easy mechanic to use when beginning game design. XP is a foundational element in many games and offers multiple options for use.

In my Realm of Nobles game, players begin with zero XP. They gain XP by doing "extra credit" projects that earn them game points but not grade points. Additionally, they can earn XP during designated days in class, which for me are simulation days. In the Realm, I use XP as the backbone of the entire game. Players work together to put their class or house on the top of the leaderboard. House totals are the sum total of all the students' individual XP in that particular class period. I use three leaderboards for my students: individual leaderboards, house leaderboards, and guild or group leaderboards. This is helpful, since a limited number of students will be at the top of the individual leaderboard. This visibility of XP (status) pushes students to work together as a whole class to ensure everyone is contributing to their house. Additionally, the teamwork fosters a sense that "we are all in this together." Students know their XP counts toward a greater goal.

XP is also used to level students up. I started off by having each 1,000 points level up my students. They were able to see where they were by checking the leaderboard. The reason they care about leveling up, other than adding more points to their house and guild, is to gain powers and abilities that will help them in the game. Like most video and board games, my game is filled with items that students can earn and then use. However, most of these items require players to be at a certain level to be able to use them.

Once you have a point structure, you will discover ways to play with these points and use them in your game. XP provides possibilities for creating an engaged learning environment. We do, however, need to be cognizant of the fact that these are really just more numbers we are giving students. We can't stop there. We need to make sure that students use these points in conjunction with other game mechanics described in this chapter to ensure they are meaningful and not just a slapped on, hollow, "gamified" experience.

LEVELS

EXPLANATION

Levels indicate a player's position or rank. A level can also refer to a player's current stage in the game.

PROS

- Fulfills Status, Access, and Power elements of Status, Access, Power, and Stuff (SAPS theory)
- The perfect complement to your XP points
- Great way to motivate deeply invested players

CONS

- Quite useless, used alone or only with points
- Can be discouraging if you don't give great care to your level structure

USES AND IDEAS

Levels can be used in several ways. They can represent where a player is in the game. For example, in the game Mario Brothers, the game designers called each level in the game a "world." You started on world one and moved up from there. A frequent question heard in my childhood neighborhood was, "What world are you on?" Your answer clearly indicated how far you progressed in the game and was a badge of honor among friends.

Another way to use levels is in conjunction with your XP. As students gain more XP, they can level up. I named my levels, and students enjoy gaining level titles and the associated powers.

Here are a few titles I use:

Newbie	Initiate	Beginner
Novice	Apprentice	Enthusiast
Craftsman	Artisan	Journeyman
Expressive	Skilled	Adept
Intermediate	Experienced	Proficient
Professional	Advanced	Specialist
Veteran	Scholar	Virtuoso
Star	Leader	Champion
Governor	Grandmaster	Master

Hattrick, a popular soccer management game[1], uses the words below to identify a player's level, skill, and abilities:

Non-existent	Disastrous	Wretched
Poor	Weak	Inadequate
Passable	Solid	Excellent
Formidable	Outstanding	Brilliant
Magnificent	World-class	Titanic
Supernatural	Mythical	Magical
Utopian	Extra-terrestrial	Divine

These are two simple examples of level structures. Let your creativity connect your level structure to your content. For example, science students could start as primordial ooze, history students could move up army ranks, English literature students could earn famous awards like Caldecott and Newbery. You can invite your students to create them as well! Once you have a theme picked out for your game, it will be easier to decide the rank titles. Feel free to borrow from games you know or the above examples.

Note: Levels can also identify an entire class or a group. Once a group or class earns enough points, their group levels up and now has abilities. To completely blow their minds, you could have all of the above layers of levels. Having potential individual levels, plus team levels, supports student motivation and team building.

LEADERBOARDS

EXPLANATION

Leaderboards show the standings for players or groups and can report both their local and global rank.

PROS

- Fulfills the status part of the SAPS theory
- Local leaderboards keep like players interested
- Can be for players, groups, or the whole class

CONS

- Total rankings can be discouraging to some of your players.
- For confidentiality reasons, leaderboards can't be made public if your game points are your grade points.

USES AND IDEAS

In my gamified course, I use leaderboards to display a ton of information. Leaderboards provide the game data necessary for players to make strategic decisions. Students are motivated by the rankings and work to stay at or near the top. Other students will enjoy setting micro-goals to work their way to higher levels.

One way to increase the powerful influence of leaderboards is to increase the information displayed. I like to give my students several data points. My leaderboards display their class total, their group total, as well as their individual total. The Realm of Nobles is a yearlong experience. As such, the leaderboard is an ongoing total of XP earned throughout the year. Some teachers structure leaderboards that only last for the unit and then reset. Resetting can be a way to reinvigorate with a new goal and a fresh start.

Another use of leaderboards is to keep track of unit rank scores and then to give items or powers based on their previous ranks. In the Realm, I don't reset their scores; however, one way I keep them excited and working hard is by displaying the quarter leaderboard. This shows what they earned in the current quarter as well as how many places they moved up or down from last quarter.

For example, during last year's game, five students stayed at the top the entire year. Other students felt they couldn't compete with them. However, when they looked at the local and quarter leaderboards, they saw several new students were in the top five for that quarter. Surpassing the top five on the overall leaderboard was not possible, due to the large amount of accumulated points in previous quarters. However, other students were able to earn more than the top five players during the current quarter, which was a motivator.

Leaderboards contribute to other game elements, like the rules. For example, maybe in a new unit you ask students to pair up with people based on their ranks on the leaderboard. Another way is to offer side quests that students can only do if they are in the top half or the bottom half. Or you can give a special ability to students that are in a certain range on the leaderboard. For example: "If you are ranked between thirty and fifty, you can do quests multiple times."

These micro-awards based on ranks can start to make it "cool" to be at those different levels. Another idea is to give different ranks to be used in a group. That way, when students are building a team, they might be inclined to select people from different rank levels because it would help the individuals as well as the group.

You can see how you are able to use points, ranks, and levels when you have a leaderboard. Set one up, even if you don't wish to make all the data public to the students. The workable data will help you create other mechanics for your game. Leaderboards are foundational to many games, which is why many game designers include them. I am confident that, if done with intention, leaderboards can be helpful and motivational for a sizable portion of your student body.

Tip: A great tool to set up your leaderboard is Google Sheets. This makes it easy to share with students if you would like.

Guilds

Explanation

Guilds are alliances of parties or small groups of people and can be formed for just about any reason. This a "fancy" name for individual student groups.

Pros

- Creates relatedness and shared game experience
- Can be a huge help to get non-gamers into your game
- Additional structure that you can use in conjunction with other game mechanics

Cons

- Forces teamwork and collaboration even when students don't want to work with others
- Requires authentic reasons for the guild to work together

Uses and Ideas

The idea of guilds is a familiar one, since students are often put into groups. In the game world, guilds encourage group members to be more like teammates rather than pre-assigned groupmates. Unfortunately in classrooms, we often put students in collaborative experiences and then distort that collaborative experience by grading them all the same, or even separately. When you think about it, that kind of grading system isn't the best way to support a shared goal or outcome for the group. Instead, it encourages them to operate as individuals within a shared activity. Game-inspired learning creates more authentic situations for students to work together effectively toward a final goal or product.

In my game, I use the term *guild*, but your groups can be called just about anything as long as they connect to your theme and setting. Here is a generic list that could help you get started.

Examples

Tribe	Clan	Guild
Nation	District	Faction
House	Family	Gangs
Cell	Brotherhood	Regiments
Civilization	Nation	Ships

I choose to engage guilds daily and provide the setting for the learning. I set the stage for this by replacing my desks with folding tables. Folding tables? I know it might sound strange, but I love them. When I am doing an activity that requires extra space or the need to shake up how we use the classroom, the tables are able to be folded up quickly and moved to create a wide-open space.

At the start of the school year, I tell students they will be doing a lot of group work. I then explain that they will be in guilds and that I only change those guilds four or five times within the year. This is an important element for students' understanding and buy-in, and it aligns more closely with what happens in life. In the business world, workmates don't change daily or weekly.

As teachers, if we talk about the importance of becoming an effective collaborator but then put students in new groups for every project, we aren't teaching them how to work together long term. Nor is this the model for most real-world situations. My family is always my family. And my work team at school, for the most part, hasn't changed much in the past seven years. To be effective in these real-life groups, we need to leverage our collective talents to maximize the success of the project.

People often ask how I decide the members of these long-lasting student groups or guilds. My method is one that varies throughout the year. Often, students come and select a playing card from my hand. Depending on the suit they draw, that is their guild. I have to tell you that every year these are my best guilds. Students like to see that I am not manipulating, forcing, or favoring any of the groups.

After the students receive their guild placement, we have a discussion about what makes a team successful. I tell the students that a baseball team doesn't pay $100 million for a well-rounded player who can play all positions. Team owners pay that top salary for a specific talent and then try to maximize that talent by placing the player where he or she thrives. The most successful teams—the ones that are unstoppable—make sure that each individual's talents work in concert toward the same goal.

This can be eye opening for students because, by default, they usually choose to fairly divide up the work. For example, each person is responsible for a slide in a presentation and, in the end, they find themselves with a Frankenstein-type presentation. However, with this new approach, they maximize their talents by putting someone in charge of the editing, another in charge of the artistic elements, and another person on the technology, while all of them work together on the research components. When they recognize the individual talents that each member brings to the group, they end up with a phenomenal product.

Another powerful discussion I have with my students about their guilds is the concept of asset-based thinking (ABT). This is the idea that we all have a talent or passion that we bring to any group. Students forget, sometimes, that their assets don't have to be school related. I urge them to consider and use their talents and interests as well.

To help them see their own strengths, I have them identify their talents and interests. We even list them on the board, while listening to each person talk about where and when they have used these talents. All of the sudden, you look around the room and everyone is sharing a story about the positive force for change that is possible when we play to our strengths. After this discussion, group work is forever changed. Students start to think about what assets are needed and how their outside interests can support classroom projects.

Another message I like to give my overachievers and slackers is simply that these will be their guilds for a long time. I look around the room and say, "For you driven students who often take over a project, do you want to do all the work for your guild for the entire quarter? If not, it is time to invest some of your time in learning what assets the other members have so that you can effectively play to their strengths." I then look around the room and say, "It is one thing to let down a group and then move on to another group. However, this is your group for the entire quarter. If you slack off now and don't pull your weight, you will have nowhere to hide for the next project. So start learning now how you can be a contributing member and maintain your commitment to the group."

Other ways to design groups later in the year use the leaderboard. I take people in the top half and pair them with the bottom half. This way each guild has contributing members in their groups. Another time, I used the results of the Bartle Test personality assessment, which identifies the player types of individual gamers. I balanced the teams by ensuring each had all four types of gamers. Last year, I combined these team-creation approaches and gave my students some agency by explaining each of the two methods and then had them select which type they wanted me to use when I built their house guilds. It was fascinating to listen to students discuss the strengths of each method and try to cajole others to adopt their way of thinking.

My last guilds of the year use a super-awesome NFL-style draft! I know that it sounds really cruel and that someone is bound to be drafted last, but it doesn't turn out that way. I have my students talk about assets again. Each one types out a standard résumé that lists their strengths as well as their areas for growth—but they don't put their name on it. They can also write about what they think they would bring to a guild. I print out all the résumés and give them to the top four students on the leaderboard. These four leaders then pore over the information to select their new guilds. It is an awesome experience to see students try to build diverse teams that will help them succeed.

ONBOARDING

EXPLANATION

Onboarding is the process of getting a player into your game world and familiarizing them with the possibilities within the game.

PROS

- Helps get people into the game
- Helps to level the playing field for players
- Can be a natural place to display some of the other game mechanics

CONS

- Some tutorials can be boring and too long. Make sure this portion of your game is truly essential. If so, then keep it short and interesting.
- Some people try to jam in all the facets of the game. You only need to give the player what they need to know for right now.

USES AND IDEAS

Whether your game is one hour or 180 days, you need to give thought to how you will explain the rules. Just like everything in this world, there are good and bad ways of explaining a game. Onboarding is an important moment that readies your students for what lies ahead. The reality is that you might have to give a short mini-lesson on your game, but the key is to keep it short. I would suggest that you think of creative ways to allow students to explore by experiencing the game and not just talking about it.

One way I do this is to start off by telling the student groups that they are on an adventure. On the screen, I have a very cool-looking castle and epic music playing in the background (elements that help set the scene for my game). Then, with drama and fanfare, I click a button and reveal their house crest and name. I try to make it a big moment. Seriously! I try to time my speech to music playing in the background, and I recite inspirational quotes and state lofty goals, all in the name of getting them excited and curious about the game. Then, I tell them a bit of the backstory about how the king is dead and how their house and guilds need to work together to rise up and take the throne.

It's in that moment, where excitement meets confusion, that I launch them in their first house challenge. I give one student a sealed letter. Inside, they find cryptic instructions. As a house, they need to figure out this message and unlock its mystery. There is a series of clues, and students have to look up information in their textbook and on the web to figure out the message that awaits them somewhere in the school. They send one messenger to retrieve it. Upon their return, an excited class surrounds the messenger and rips open the envelope. Inside, they find a link to a Google form where they can officially enter the Realm by filling in their names, house, and guild name. I copy and paste that data into my leaderboard spreadsheet and then award each student his or her first XP. Seeing the leaderboard brings on a whole new round of awesome questions from the students.

Once they have a few points on the board, they want to know how long it takes to level up and if we will really be playing this all year. That enthusiasm is the goal! Getting them playing, even before they have all the details, gets them engaged and excited about the game and my class. Rather than giving your students all the rules, give them a compelling reason to learn the system!

The next day, students arrive to class half excited and half expecting the fun to be over. They are dead wrong. We kick off the day with team-building activities, such as the marshmallow challenge, within their guilds. (Tom Wujec delivers an excellent TED Talk about how the marshmallow challenge brings cohesion to a team. It's a great presentation and well worth watching.[2]) The team-building activity helps them bond as guilds and gives me an opportunity to introduce another feature of the game: badges. Before the activity starts, I explain what I am looking for as they build. I simply say that I want to see effective communication and inclusive actions that keep everyone working toward the goal. When I see a student doing something that fits these, I hand them a badge, explain why they got it, and then I hand them some tape and tell them to tape it to the front of their class binder.

It is a sight to see; they are proud! Heck, even their guild is proud that one of their members did a good job. By publicly explaining what the student did to earn the badge, others learn how they can earn badges—and what to do with the badges when they receive them.

Next, I teach students about the game's side quests. I don't spend too much time discussing them. I just show them where to find them and that I want them to do their best. I also let students know they are only allowed to attempt a side quest once per unit. In every class, there are those students who love to explore or overachieve. These are your early adopters. They will go home on the first night and complete one of the side quests. When they hand in their project the next day, I give them an item and a case to keep the item in. I use cards and baseball card binder sheets. (See Chapter Eight: Tools and Treasure for more information on badges and items.) At this point, I give the rest of the students an empty case (baseball card holder). Again, learning by discovery is much more fun and interesting than listening to a really long lecture.

However you do your onboarding, the important part is that you give thought to how students will learn what they need to know to play your game. Feel free to type up some of the rules for the game. I would suggest that you make a Google document that you can share. At the top of the doc, be sure to include a disclaimer stating that you can change these rules at any time.

Let your kids know up front that you have not play-tested this game. Set the expectation that, as the game master, you will need to make adjustments. It really isn't a big deal, and for the most part, all the students will understand that you will have to do this from time to time. Just make sure that when you do make changes, you are always perceived as fair. Explaining your reason for making a change helps to soften the blow.

ACHIEVEMENT

EXPLANATION

An achievement is anything that is unlocked through gameplay. In many games, achievements take on the form of badges or items.

PROS

- Gives players a sense of curiosity
- Can be beneficial for both status and exploration
- Great place for some creativity and humor

CONS

- If you use too few, you are not allowing students to have a sense of achievement.
- If you use too many, you dilute the achievement by making it seem commonplace.
- Badges alone make gamification hollow. Achievements need to be used with other mechanics.

USES AND IDEAS

Achievements can take many forms, like badges and items for example. An achievement occurs any time someone unlocks a level or the entrance to a new path or gains additional powers. Achievements give your students a sense of agency and accomplishment.

Using the path idea as an example, students would have to decide which path they think would be best for them to take. Have them piece together information to make that decision. You can raise the stakes for teams by requiring students to collect the necessary information and bring it back to their group; a group can't proceed until it has completed all the separate tasks. To keep the students motivated, I sometimes have special paths that you can only go on if you have earned a certain badge. This then leads to additional ways to earn badges by completing your chosen path.

You can also limit the choices of quests they can go on until they unlock a certain amount of the required ones. Tying achievement awards to progress can be really fun to play with and can take many forms. It can also create a sense of status, since more options are available to students who have explored deeper into the game world.

I find achievement especially fun to design because it encourages playful planning and creativity. I structure some of my units around having certain badges, collecting particular items, and exploring world history through one's own talents. Don't think of a badging system as only involving extrinsic motivation. Badges represent a roadmap of students' achievements similar to a résumé.

Badges

Let's explore badges more deeply, since they are a very well-known type of achievement in gamification. Badges are earned after successful completion of particular tasks.

In the Realm, I use two types of badges: leader badges and mini-badges. Leader badges are used for exceptional side quests. They are not limited and can be earned multiple times by the same person, if they continue to do fantastic side quests. Mini-badges are earned in class and don't require the student to do much more than complete the class activity with excellence.

As explained in the onboarding mechanics section, I use badges to get more and more students into the game. Students who choose to only engage in the class activity are still a part of the game. You can also use the mini-badges to promote general course expectations—solid group work, active listening, completion of homework, or being a top achiever—whatever works for your class goal and school initiative.

Badges work well as a micro-credentialing system, as used in Boy and Girl Scouts. When a troop member demonstrates that they have developed mastery of a certain task, they earn a badge to display this mastery.

The ability to display knowledge, like a trophy case for example, is a strong motivator for students. We already celebrate the big successes, like becoming valedictorian and winning sport championships. Yet for many students, these opportunities aren't attainable, which means some students are never recognized. As we've discussed, students love to explore both the course and how their talents perform in it. Badges are a great way to recognize each student's unique achievements.

In my game, each badge is worth XP, which is unknown to students. I don't tell students this detail because my game is yearlong, and I want to avoid what I call the *jeopardy effect*. The jeopardy effect happens when players realize there is no way their team can win, so they stop playing effectively. If I based the winner of my game only on XP, which is public information, houses could get discouraged and not try as hard. An easy fix is to give badges hidden point values that only get totaled in the end of the quarter or year. It is a great way to add mystery to your game as well.

It's important to create many different kinds of achievements. Having a variety adds to the fun and provides opportunities to tie in other game elements. For example, in my Rome unit, I wanted students to try several side quests, which I themed around the end of the triumvirate. Their goal was to collect all three badges of the Roman leaders that made up the triumvirate. By earning all three of them, the achievement added XP to each badge they earned throughout the year when I totaled them up at the end. Even though they don't know the values of each badge, they are motivated to get the triumvirate set. Not many students will earn all three, so this achievement is a huge advantage for both their house and each player personally.

POWER UPS

EXPLANATION
These provide a temporary boost for your character.

PROS
- Encourages action
- Provides status, access, and power

CONS
- If not done thoughtfully, power ups can destabilize the game and create a sense of unfairness. Students call this "OP," which stands for overpowered! Be careful to make sure your power ups are fair and balanced in your game world.

USES AND IDEAS
In the classic Nintendo game, Mario's star is a great example of a power up. The star turned on special music and made your character flash. You were invincible because you could run really fast and bump into your enemies and WIN! The game masters balanced this power by making it temporary; it only lasted for about thirty seconds at a time.

Another power up example from Mario is the mushroom. The mushroom turned Mario into a larger version of himself. The empowered Mario could break blocks by hitting them, and if he bumped into an enemy, he didn't die but shrunk back down to his normal size.

In the uses and ideas sections that follow, I will provide suggestions for power ups that will enhance particular mechanics or benefit the class in general. For example, you could use power ups to encourage more side quests or to increase class participation in the next day's discussions. These experiences support a variety of learning opportunities for all students.

Quests

Explanation

A quest is a mission with an objective.

Pros

- Great way to reward students for their exploration & mastery
- Can fulfill status and access (SAPS)
- A great structural way to move students through your game/course

Cons

- Quests take time to develop. *Tip*: Start with projects you already have and just apply your new theme to it.
- Can take time to test and lay out
- They need to be worth doing to ensure teacher and student motivation.

Uses and Ideas

Quests form the heart of many games. Think of creative names for quests that will follow your game's theme and setting.

Here are some possible ideas:

Tasks	Missions	Sorties
Trials	Adventures	Voyages
Hunts	Commissions	Cases
Investigations	Experiments	Raids
Expeditions	Patrols	Safaris
Treks	Journeys	Races
Battles	Events	

In my game, quests are optional, so I call them "side quests." I suggest you post quests on a learning management system (LMS) like Edmodo, Moodle, or Schoology. When I post quests, I also explain that students can earn XP, items, or badges by completing them.

Part of the purpose of side quests is to help students become more self-directed. For that reason, I intentionally make my quests incredibly open-ended. I want students to discover that, if they put in the effort, they can learn just about anything. I don't spell out all the ways to complete a quest. No rubric is provided, just a set of simple directions and a few rules that apply to all my quests:

1. All side quest topics must deal with the current unit.
2. Each quest can only be turned in once.
3. All quests have to be turned in before the end of a unit.
4. Additional requirements will be posted on quest directions if needed.

These four simple rules unleash students' motivations and untethered creativity. On average, 75 percent of my class attempts side quests per unit. In case you're curious, here is my rationale for the side quest rules:

RULE ONE: ALL SIDE QUESTS MUST BE TOPICS THAT RELATE TO THE CURRENT UNIT.

I want my students to engage with the content at a deeper level—beyond the standards—through the side quest challenge. This allows them to authentically participate and even lead class discussions on main topics and learning objectives. For this reason, they can only use the content in our current unit.

Additional Power Available: Create a power or item that allows students to go back to previous units—maybe for comparison or to deepen understanding.

Rule Two: Each quest can only be turned in once.

Originally, I didn't have this rule because, when I created side quests, I assumed students who chose to do them would take their time and carefully craft their quests. Most kids gave their best effort, but the rule was needed because a handful raced through all of them and earned very little XP. I wanted to encourage them to do their very best, instead of turning in tons of junk. Setting that rule was a positive step in helping students focus more on quality and getting it right.

Additional Power Up Ideas: With this rule you can have several powers:

- Allow a student to get a preview of possible points earned.
- Allow for them to do a quest twice (great if there is a type of quest that students like to do).
- Allow a student to redo quests (could be a limited power or unlimited).

Rule Three: All quests must be turned in before the end of a unit.

I added this rule so that students would have some sense of urgency. As my quests are optional, I wanted to make sure that students had a reason to pace out their work and get it done. By having this urgency built into the game, it helps students think about time management, which every sixth grader is developing and will carry well beyond the year.

Additional Power Up Ideas: A simple idea is the ability to turn in quests late. You could keep it wide open or limit the number of days they are allowed to still submit it.

Rule Four: Additional requirements will be posted on quest directions if needed.

This is the catch-all rule. On each of my posted quests, I have a requirements section. Here, I might put something simple like "The final project must be emailed to me." Sometimes, I add additional requirements, like stating that the quest must be done with a team of four people. I also find it motivating for students to adjust the difficulty level. So, I might require that the quest is done with a group of people who are all in different classes or in different sections of the leaderboard. This creates diversity and can even bring new people into the game.

Additional Power Up Ideas: Create a power up that allows students to disregard the additional rules. One power my students love is the ability to change one word or to add or subtract one number from the additional requirement sentences. Students love these creative power ups and have fun seeing where they can be applied.

ITEMS

EXPLANATION

An item is anything that a player wears or can use for a power up or additional ability.

PROS

- Can create endless experiences in your game
- Creates a unique personalization within the game, which means every character will have different powers due to their items.
- Fulfills status, access, and power of the SAPS theory
- Just plain fun!

CONS

- Need to make sure the drop percentage isn't too low or too high.
- Takes time to create and manage… but it's so worth it!

Uses and Ideas

Items, along with power ups, are my personal favorite mechanic to use. They really get the students excited and create the true sense of existing in a game. The possibilities for the kinds of items you will create are endless. If you are constructing a short game that is applied to a unit, you will want to create all the items before your game is launched. However, if you are building a yearlong game, your items will be built over time and take on a life of their own as the game progresses. Each year, I add more and more items to my game.

Items can be tangible things a player picks up or earns as the game progresses. Some items are essential to future challenges, while others just provide a boost and make life easier and more fun. My items are slips of paper with cool graphics and an explanation of what the item does. Below are some examples of items that can be earned in my game. I explain these items, as well as many others, in the Tools and Treasure Chest chapter.

Items in connection with power ups can bend rules and create new currencies. (See "Currency" on page 108.) Rules for items in my game are quite simple. All players receive one baseball card holder sheet to keep in their binders; all items must be stored in the card holder. This limits the number of items they can hold and creates interesting game choices for students. Another rule is that items cannot stack, which means that if you have several of the same items, they will each get their own pocket. This rule helped me manage items faster as I could easily see what powers students had at any given moment. I also created this rule so that later items could break that rule. For example, the sword rack allows a student to stack level-one swords and spears in one pocket. Many students liked having these, as it allowed them to hold many more items.

Once you create items, you will use more mechanics from this chapter. When you start to create items, connect them to your class for a more personal and immersive experience. Items will help you take advantage of your classroom environment as well as help you adapt your teaching style to fit the game theme and setting.

When I first sat down to create items, it was the single hardest part of game design. I struggled with what to give students, especially because I didn't want them to affect the class grade all that much. To overcome the challenge, I first attacked the low-hanging fruit by making items for locker passes and late homework.

When my creative well ran dry, I had to trust that ideas for items would come as the game developed. As I experienced classroom

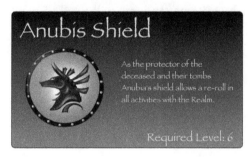

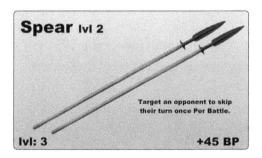

gameplay, I was able to create more and more items. Recurring events that unfolded in my class—like test review days, team challenges, essays, projects, and side quests— inspired me to create a flood of items that related to game rules and activities. In the Realm, for example, the spear allows you to skip a team's turn during a review game. This item doesn't cost me anything or give the students any grade advantage; it is just plain old fun!

Take courage! You will dive deep into items once you use other mechanics, choose course events, and build the game rules. Then you can decide which items students will need to playfully learn the content.

Skills

Explanation
Skills are characteristics of players that can grow through gameplay.

Pros
- Fulfills status, access, and power of SAPS theory
- Creates meaningful game choices for students

Cons
- Can create imbalance in the game if all skills are not equally powerful

Uses and Ideas
Skills are foundational to many games. The game Diablo, for example, asks players to make a major decision right from the load screen. Players have to select a character class before they embark on the epic 100+ hour adventure that is the game. The choices are barbarian, wizard, and monk. Each of these characters comes with special benefits that only they can earn or unlock, as they gain experience and level up. Once the player selects his or her character class, there is no changing

it; it represents the player for the entirety of the game and determines what he or she can do.

If you don't like the idea of using items in your game, skills are another great way to go. Skills and items can also be used together to create a rich learning environment. Skills, though more challenging to create, are in many ways easier to manage. Character skills are a "cool" addition to any game, as they provide reasons for students to collaborate in teams that benefit one another.

A word of caution: In my opinion, it can be incredibly hard to make a skills chart for your first game. Each of the character types needs to be balanced and worth choosing. You won't be able to adjust the character classes once you start, as students can't switch; they will protest if they determine their choice would have been different had they known what the abilities would become.

An educational resource that uses skills really well is Classcraft. com In this game, each of the characters has abilities that can help each member of the group. Students should be encouraged naturally by the game to make sure they have a player representing each skill type.

By having different types of players, you are creating a collaborative experience for your students and an opportunity for them to be proud of the leveling up of their character.

For those of you struggling with the difference between items and skills, there is little to none. Take the spear item we looked at before, which has the power to skip a team's turn during a review game. In a skills-based game, this power is earned by leveling up one's character type. I have toyed with the idea of making a power up chart for each of my classes that students can select from and create unique classroom powers as their house total XP increases. Again, the chief concern is making sure the characters are balanced.

Currency

Explanation

Currency can be anything that can be accumulated to gain a benefit, like points, that can be traded for items.

Pros

- Fulfills status and power of SAPS theory
- Enhances the economic system of your game
- Can help infuse more interest in long-term games

Cons

- Totally useless if your game doesn't have an economy
- These need to have more advanced mechanics at play.
- Can be hard to balance and maintain

Uses and Ideas

Currency in its most basic form is often some kind of money that can be collected and traded in to buy something. In my class, one of the currencies is gold. It allows them to buy items in my game world. This can be a very fun element and one that allows for action to happen that motivates learning. A common lesson students have to learn is determining the difference between a need and a want and making decisions accordingly. Talk about life skills!

Here are a few things to consider:

1. Is it manageable? How much time will it involve?

As with all game elements, you have to think about your time. What you expend to manage any game mechanic or tool needs to be worth the gains in student motivation and learning. For me, the currency of gold in my game is worth the trouble. I have a spreadsheet to keep track of their earnings. The shop is simply a single webpage that shows what the shopkeeper has in stock. Students select what game item they wish to purchase and click the email order button (see no. 3 below). During the workday, I fly through the orders and subtract their money. It's quick and easy. While it would be cool to have physical currency that students could trade with one another, I decided keeping it digital was much easier to manage and still supported the positive outcomes.

2. CAN STUDENTS CHEAT?

I hate to ask this question, but in my experience when it comes to money, there is a high temptation for students to cheat. As such, I decided early on to give students very little control over the currency. Please feel empowered to choose differently! For me, the trouble of making sure no one was cheating wasn't worth having the currency. This is also the reason why I manage it digitally. On my spreadsheet, students can see how much they have to spend before making purchases. As for trading, they can't do that with money; however, with my game's array of items, there are plenty of things they can trade without currency.

3. DO I HAVE THINGS FOR THEM TO BUY?

I like to structure my game so that students are not earning anything of real market value. I believe that making the available sale items relevant to the game world creates more authentic gameplay and encourages intrinsic play rather than extrinsic rewards. Skillful gameplay is intrinsic; cheap prizes are extrinsic. By focusing on the skills and learning, we are bringing back the true power of play in our classrooms. When you set up a "shop," consider offering personal items, group items, and class items for sale. These multiple levels create interesting gameplay.

While currency can be defined in a narrow scope of "something that can be used to buy goods and services," we can widen that definition in the game. Let's think of currency as anything that can be collected, measured, and ultimately used in some fashion. When I did my first gamified unit around the Greek Olympics, I only had one currency, Olympic Points, which weren't money. Students worked to collect the points that could be used to win the game.

When I started to build my yearlong game, I only had one currency, experience points or XP. For the first few weeks, this was enough. Then I noticed that some students were excited about the game for reasons beyond collecting XP. So this led me to consider other possible currencies that would add dimension to the game. It didn't take me long to land on the idea of gold. It supported the storyline and was manageable for me.

Eventually, I created two more currencies: tools and battle points. "Tools" became another item that could be earned and spent to upgrade several items or buildings in the game. I was amazed at how much this added to the game for the students. While many still loved and were interested in leveling up and earning XP, other students enjoyed exploring the possibilities of this new currency.

Battle Points, or BP, supported the setting in the Middle Ages. I added some cool weapons as the items they could purchase. I didn't want them to do damage to each other, so I limited the choices of what could be done with weapons in the game. Then the idea came that BP would work like XP. Students would collect items that have a BP value in their binders that, when totaled, could be used in different ways. I share this information to show you how, once you have a game mechanic, you will be able to design many more items and powers to use with it.

Another way I use BP is during a review game. I have students total up their guild's BP and use that as their starting score in our review game. Remember, these items are earned by going on side quests in my game. I love how, during review games, some guilds have more points due to the fact they have quested more and, as such, are seasoned veterans. Students see the link between work during the unit and their abilities at the end of the unit. This is a powerful message to reinforce for our students.

BP can also be used on tests. BP doesn't help their academic score; however, when the tests are battles, each correctly answered question is a strike against the enemy. The enemy could be another team or just a fake army they must defeat by earning enough BP. I've also had the classes (houses) compete against one another. The class that earns the most BP wins the battle. Each student writes their BP total at the top of the test, and I calculate the total points earned for the class. Using BP this way shows students that sometimes we need to work together to defeat the external enemy.

You can see by these examples that game currencies don't always have to be money. If you have a larger game, I would consider having a variety of currencies to increase students' critical thinking and motivation to engage more fully in the learning experience.

CASCADING INFORMATION THEORY

EXPLANATION

Only essential information is provided at intentional points during the game narrative to ensure that just the right amount of understanding is gained to affect gameplay.

PROS

- Fulfills a sense of curiosity and an eagerness to stay engaged
- Prevents students getting bogged down with irrelevant information

CONS

- It's hard to perfect. Too much or too little information can have negative effects.
- It can be hard for teachers to surrender to the natural state of being the learner as they explore. We naturally want to teach rather than allow discovery and whatever accompanies it.

Uses and Ideas

Game designers use this powerful mechanic on both the micro and macro levels of their games. The idea is simple—give players just the right amount of information to feel comfortable and able to succeed without droning on to the point that details become insignificant.

On the macro level, I don't know a single large video game that tries to lay out all the rules before play. Instead, designers embed the need-to-know concepts as players progress in the game. They incorporate discovery in the learning process by making it active and sometimes challenging.

The thing that game designers recognize is that nothing will stop a player who has a compelling reason to learn. In the game environment, when players (or students) have natural questions, or want to do something in a different way, they seek out the information to execute the new idea.

This is where I stand on my soapbox and say that educators must clue into this truth about learning. Instead of drowning our students with rules, rubrics, and rhetoric, we should allow them to discover content and standards through playful learning.

You don't have
to have the entire game all planned
out from the first day of play.

What does this look like in schools? For starters, it doesn't mean abandoning student instruction through lectures or mini-lessons. The point of this mechanic is to learn the joy of discovery. Our courses are rich with content and lessons that, I believe, students should be allowed to discover. Our methods, such as gamification, can serve as tools that help students internalize and construct meaning from the learning.

By keeping information sessions short and simple, you allow space for students to be creative. At the same time, because you haven't told them everything, they are motivated to become independent learners and discover what they need to move forward in the game. Excitement accompanies working through a problem and gaining understanding on the other side of mastery. Mastery is gained; it isn't given, inferred, or disseminated. This is a core principle of game design. We must allow students to struggle through the learning of the game at just the right level of frustration.

Embrace the notion that not all information needs to be given to your students at one time. (That gives you some freedom and flexibility too. You don't have to have the entire game all planned out from the first day of play.) At the start of the unit or year, your students will have unanswered questions. That's great! Curiosity will keep them engaged with the game, the course, and their own thinking. Students love this mechanic; it allows discovery, new opportunities, and widens their eyes with endless possibilities.

Micro-Challenges and Mini-Games

Explanation
These mini-moments bring game elements together through an intriguing new dynamic.

Pros
- Helpful to bring students together
- Something different and new—adds excitement!
- Creative space to think about different ways to shake it up!

Cons
- If you keep having the same challenges, it can be repetitive and boring.
- It can be hard to keep coming up with new ideas.

Uses and Ideas

Micro-challenges and mini-games can come in many forms. For example, they could be a review game or a team-building exercise. I offer several of these mini-moments, and most of them center around the following key principles of mini-challenges in full-production video games:

1. Mini-challenges don't have to fit the overarching story line.
2. Mini-challenges produce a quick sense of accomplishment.
3. Mini-challenges serve to help the larger game.

When designing a challenge or doing a mini-game for your classroom, be cognizant of the overall user experience. Does it look like you need to shake things up? Do you need to add a bit of pop to the class? Are there certain skills you need to reinforce, and is there a creative way you could do it?

Challenges are a great way to bring a team or class together to work on a common problem. In one mini-challenge I created to review course content, I had students create a mural on a six-foot piece of butcher paper. The mural had to cover the entire space and represent the information covered in the chapter. Because they only had one class period to complete it, everyone had to be involved.

It was a phenomenal activity! At first, the class went into chaos; students didn't know who should do what. I hadn't done a whole-class challenge since the beginning of the year, and the students wanted me to take control. For a moment, I thought the mini-challenge was going to be a complete bust. Then, a few natural leaders rose up and helped create order and direction. This happened in every class. The leaders divided students into sub-teams, each with a task to complete. One group, the research group, was charged with looking through the chapter to make sure all the key elements got covered. Then there was the pre-draw team. These students put the researched ideas into concepts that could be sketched on the mural. These concepts were then handed to the artistic director who worked with the "graffiti" artists who were in charge of bringing the stick figure concepts to life on the mural. Then there was the rainbow group that added color to the sketches on the mural. There were, of course, several supervisors who, I might add, were some of the best supervisors I have ever seen. These leaders really did a great job of floating from group to group, meeting each group's needs, and filling in shortcomings where they could. I saw leaders work side by side with all those stations. All of these categories and divisions of labor were student generated and directed.

In the end, all the classes finished their murals, which were filled with wonderful ideas and creative flairs. However, the full impact of the activity was that students learned how to work as a large, effective team. We hung each one in the classroom as banners of honor. The students were so proud of what they had created together.

Providing mini-challenges like this helps solidify the content acquisition. It also builds students' confidence, communication skills, and resiliency—life skills that will benefit them well beyond the activity.

Mini-games and challenges like these shake up students' cognitive and social routines and hit the reset button on their course expectations. I love seeing students think differently. These challenges require them be flexible and behave more intentionally.

LIFE JACKETS

EXPLANATION

This can be a framework or tool that helps players progress in the game or catch up if they are too far behind.

PROS

- Helps move more players into the game
- Makes the game more competitive as all could still win
- Can be a source of great encouragement
- Brings about positive uncertainty

Cons

- Might discourage top players who don't gain many life jackets
- Need to make sure what you do is still seen as fair

Uses and Ideas

Life jackets are similar to a scaffolded unit design. As a game mechanic, life jackets are public information. Often, utilizing a life jacket is a strategic move to let other players know you got an advantage. In the classroom setting, this is more challenging to embrace since we often emphasize fairness for the whole class rather than fairness for the whole child.

A famous game principle that I talk about with my students is the Mario Kart effect. Mario Kart, a racing game with power ups, is not only fun but unfair. Why then is it one of the most popular and best-selling franchises on the Nintendo platform? It's simple—Mario Kart uses power ups as life jackets to help struggling players remain with the pack. At the same time, it also makes the game more and more difficult for the front-runner.

Every year, I unpack this concept with my students by asking why a game would be intentionally unfair. The students all know the right answers. They say, "Because it makes it more fun for both." The bottom player will lose by just a little bit, maybe even doing well enough to win, which keeps them coming back for more. The top player can also be proud of the narrow victory and of the fact that, even with the game stacked against him, he was still able to succeed.

I tell my students that I want our game to be like that game. I promise to be fair in my unfairness. This always gets a chuckle from the kids. But honestly, I think they understand that a good game is one in which everyone has a chance when they focus, collaborate, and most importantly give it their all.

Because some players take longer to get into the game than others, it's important to provide a way to allow them, through hard work, to remain with the pack. This also keeps all players on their toes, so to speak. The bottom players, by upping their game, can take a solid run at the players ahead of them. At the same time, the players above them need to be diligent and keep plugging away to avoid a slip in the rankings.

I provide life jackets for my students through all sorts of methods. I create items to provide critical information at valuable moments. Other times, I provide the ability to check out an informative textbook. I insert XP doublers and even multipliers that help students with lower points. These advantages are only available through gameplay, which means students must be applying themselves or taking risks in the game and with the content in order to receive the life jacket. When students understand from the beginning that life jackets are not free, they collectively share in a sense of relief.

QUICK IDEAS FOR LIFE JACKETS:
- Items that give more XP or time on assignments, challenges, or quests
- Score lower players more XP and higher students with less.
- Have some quests that are only available to the lower half of the leaderboard. Give the upper half of the leaderboard a chance to earn an item that would also unlock these quests for them.

PvP OR PLAYER VERSUS PLAYER

EXPLANATION
PvP is any kind of event that puts players in direct conflict or competition, from tournaments to one-on-one brawls.

Pros

- Source of status
- Adds real chance of failure as only one team can win
- Should have this element at least once in the year

Cons

- Can be too competitive
- If you don't control this aspect of your game, students can take it too far.
- Balance is essential.
- Can make less competitive players flee

Uses and Ideas

Player versus player, at first glance, may seem like something we wouldn't want to include in our classrooms. Done right, however, it can add a whole new dimension to the game. It doesn't have to be one student versus another; competition can be between teams or even whole classes. The key component when employing the PvP mechanic is that something valuable is either earned or risked.

One way to set up group competitions is with Kahoot!, a free web tool. You can create a trivia game that allows limitless numbers of players at a time. Students receive a code to join the current game in which they can buzz in with their answers to earn points. Each question is worth 1,000 points, and the points decrease the longer it takes them to answer the question.

During my Rome unit, I used gladiator fights in the coliseum to integrate PvP into my game. During the Kahoot! Gladiator Challenges, I allowed students to challenge each other. I had my students log in with a number before their name, e.g. 7 Michael or 12 Heidi. Students who were challenging each other put the same number before their name. This allowed me to have multiple challenges happening simultaneously. When the game was over, I downloaded and sorted the results to see who won each of the challenges. In one round of Kahoot!

Gladiator Challenges, I could settle dozens of competitions.

Being based on real gladiator combat, these fights are to the death. When students lose, they write their names on the "Wall of the Fallen" and are no longer able to challenge anyone. Kids loved coming in at recess or before school to do the Kahoot! challenges. Students could decide both who to play and how many players to challenge. I told them that the emperor wanted to see interesting battles. With each win, they earned XP, and the better the game, the more XP they earned. This PvP is a good example of having the right elements to make the game work. Students risk losing the chance to earn XP or hidden items from the emperor, and they enjoyed the control of choosing opponents. For PvP, this tool provides just the right amount of tension.

COMMUNAL DISCOVERY

EXPLANATION

Communal Discovery occurs when the entire community pulls together to overcome a challenge or solve a problem.

PROS

- Immensely viral and very fun
- Builds teamwork and a sense of accomplishment for all
- Can bring more players deeper into your game world

CONS

- Complex to build but totally worth it!

USES AND IDEAS

A communal discovery is an event that players need to work together to solve. It is a great bonding point in any game because it increases teamwork and unites players in the game. When all players are pulled into an event, even your least invested player starts to feel connected to something bigger. After an event like this one, I see an uptick in other game-related activities as well as content acquisition. Simply put, students are more into the game and the course itself after an event like this.

In my course, I structure my Greek test as a battle between Greece and Persia. All the houses need to work together to score the points necessary to defeat the Persians. I have had students create spontaneous study groups, share notes via Google Docs, and hold Skype study sessions, all of which fostered a sense of community.

Real-life escape games, called Breakout Rooms, are another example of the communal discovery mechanic. The idea behind escape games is that a team is locked in a room and, together, must use the clues hidden in the room to escape in less than sixty minutes.

You can create this game on your own or purchase a kit from BreakoutEDU.com, a new company that has created a way to apply this game mechanic to your class content. The kit includes a series of locks and boxes. Students need to solve the first clue to unlock the first lock. Once they do, they might find other clues to the puzzle, which lead to further clues that eventually help them achieve the overall goal. They have forty-five minutes to work together to get this done. It is a phenomenal experience that students will be talking about long after the course is done.

TIME EVENTS

EXPLANATION

Time Events are moments in the game that incorporate a time constraint; timed missions and speed quests are examples.

PROS

- Fulfills curiosity and status
- Creates a feeling of losing stuff and avoidance
- Great to gather people

Cons

- If no one is aware the activity is posted, then it's a lost opportunity.
- If time is too long, there is no incentive. You have to get the time just right to be motivating. Incorporate too much or too little, and the activity loses effectiveness.

Uses and Ideas

This is one of my favorite mechanics to add to a game when it is running a little flat. The concept is simple, and students engage quickly. It's also a perfect mechanic when you have a content task you need to get done and only so much time to do it.

The LEGO Challenge is one way I've employed this mechanic, and it's a student favorite. For this challenge, you'll need basic LEGO sets that include several standard blocks as well as mini-figures. Give each group a LEGO set and instruct them to build three scenes from that day's homework, reading, or flipped video. The students have thirty minutes to build. Then they take photos of their LEGO creations and do a voiceover to present important information from the assignment.

This is gamification at its best! "It is challenging, and at moments the task may seem impossible. Then, because of the challenge, they start to work together and think strategically about tasks and resources. At the start, students can only use blocks that are in their kits. After a while, I announce that some of the teams, due to their good collaborative efforts and effective communication skills, have earned the use of miniature figurines. They then clamor to go get the "perfect" ones for their scenes. In later challenges, I add other elements, such as the gong. When I ring the gong, students must work together in silence until I ring it again.

As you can see, I took a basic idea, like reading homework review, and layered in game elements that require teamwork and application of content knowledge. Throughout the year, I make the task harder and harder, and the students love it more and more.

Think of dressing up your next timed activity by simply adding a large timer up on your board. Google timer sunsets are one of my favorites to project onto the classroom screen. When I tell students they need to finish before sundown, they immediately get to work. It is an entertaining motivator for me and the students.

Another way to use the time mechanic is through the appointment dynamic. Your local pub's "happy hour" is an example of this mechanic. In the classroom, students receive a certain bonus for being somewhere at a certain time. For example, I post quick-quests online that have a twenty-four hour, or less, window for completion. Bonus: it promotes frequent checking of my class learning management system.

Another example of the appointment dynamic is trivia night. I use Celly, a program that allows you to make a private social network, to have an online chat discussion. One evening I thought, "Let's see how many students might show for an impromptu trivia game." I announced the 7:00 p.m. trivia game to students using Celly and noted that all were welcome to participate online. With only a two-hour advance notice, thirty students showed up!

We played the trivia game using the online, closed social network of Celly, since it works on any phone, tablet or computer. I explained that I would post questions in the typical Q1/A1 style. All correct answers submitted before I asked the next question would earn points. The game lasted an hour. I learned the next day that some of the students were even playing as a family. At school, all the kids were abuzz about the impromptu trivia night. They were asking when the next one was and made me promise there would be other similar activities.

This event illustrates the engaging power of gamification integrated into course content. The students were essentially begging me for another night of studying because the learning involved motivating game elements that made the task of studying FUN!

PUNISHMENT

EXPLANATION

Penalties to players that provide a way to stabilize your game

PROS

- Can engage players through avoidance of these penalties (use cautiously)
- Increasing the risk will increase engagement in a game.
- Can help balance out the game

CONS

- Positive feedback is always better than negative feedback.
- If not done right, it can really ruin players' interest in engaging with the game.
- I wouldn't use it if your game is tied to grades; that is already high stakes.
- Use with caution.

USES AND IDEAS

The punishment mechanic isn't as evil as it sounds. Many games use this element because it helps rebalance the game after extended play. It is found in many economics-based games, such as the early versions of SimCity.

The challenge in SimCity is to develop a thriving city. At first, you have a very limited amount of cash, so you need to balance your growth very carefully. However, like most of these economic games, once your city has "made it" and has plenty of cash flow, the game isn't as fun to play. Essentially, it has become too easy.

In later iterations of the game, the designers added more and more challenges, like political demands and natural disasters as a city grew. It was painful, but honestly more fun. Additionally, the designers were able to rebalance the system by forcing players to spend more money as they advanced; the demands made money rare and more desirable.

I use the punishment mechanic for similar reasons. For example, an item that students can earn early in the game is the Neolithic spear. The spear has minimal status and are cheap to obtain. However, at the start of the game, this item is really good because possessing items is uncommon. By the time second quarter rolls around, the market is flooded with these lame spears. To rebalance the game, I start introducing several mechanics that will clear out the market glut of the spears. I use a mini-challenge review session where, if a group or a student gets a question wrong, they lose an item. I am the one who selects that item, and this is when I take away the items that need thinning out.

Another option is to change the value of an item through the storyline. For example, when I began my unit on Egypt, as part of the story, I said that Ramses the Great was preparing for a huge battle with the Hittites and needed all the items possible. The guilds and houses that turned in the most items (spears for example) would gain the Pharaoh's favor. This meant that if your house or guild gifted to the Pharaoh the highest quantity of the requested item, spears in our example, the guild or house would gain something special. The converse was also true. If students turned in the least of the given item, the Pharaoh wouldn't be pleased at all. This twist in a game mechanic puts a common and unimportant item at the center of the game. Students were now clamoring to get their hands on spears and making secret offerings to the Pharaoh to ensure that they were in the lead.

In both of these examples, the punishment mechanic wasn't too harsh and didn't really discourage gameplay. In the second case, it even fueled them to work harder.

I've used the following examples of the punishment mechanic in my class to encourage positive outcome and address issues, like missing homework, in a way that supports students working together. Thinking as a game designer, I want to move students toward homework completion and use this mechanic to move students toward action.

In general, each example below is a temporary, fun challenge mechanic, rather than a standing classroom rule.

Most Missing

The class with the most missing assignments is unable to have a Realm day. Realm days are a big deal in my classroom, as these are the days that I "pay out" side quests, give students the things they bought in the shop, and allow students to upgrade their items. It is fair to say they never want to miss a Realm day. When I used this mechanic, I saw my students transform right before my eyes. Students formed TAC or Teach, Advise, Coach models. The idea was simple: form TACs in pairs. The partners pushed each other to do their best in class and get late work completed. Students came up with this peer coaching on their own because in order to succeed, they needed to support one another.

Labor Lost

This is a way for classes to interact with one another. The houses gained points, 500 XP, per missing assignment difference between each of the classes.

Example:

Class one: Missing two assignments

Class two: Missing five assignments

Class three: Missing six assignments

Class four: Missing ten assignments

Class one earns +1500 points from class two, +2000 points from class three and +4000 points from class four. Total earned: 7500XP

Class two earns: -1500 from class one, +500 from class three and +2500 points from class four. Total earned: +1500

CLASS THREE EARNS: -2000 FROM CLASS ONE, -500
POINTS FROM CLASS TWO, AND + 2000 FROM CLASS
FOUR. TOTAL: -500

CLASS FOUR EARNS: -4000 FROM CLASS ONE, -2500
FROM CLASS TWO, AND -2000 FROM CLASS THREE.
TOTAL: -8500 POINTS.

This mechanic was fun as it encouraged teams to turn in their work in order to earn more points. Take a look at class three for example. They have six missing assignments; if they turn in one assignment, that would turn their -500 into +1500 points.

Again, students liked this model and encouraged others to get their work done. They understood that missing work hurt the overall house. They worked as an entire house to get these students to bring their work in and helped make sure future work was on time and done correctly.

THE KEEPER

This one twists the other two on their heads. At the start of a unit, I give out a badge or item and give it a power or value that would work with the game. Then I put in place a few rules for the Keeper challenge. Each time someone has a missing assignment, they lose their Keeper badge. If the class loses five of them, they all lose them. Another way to do this is to require that students have a certain number of Keeper badges to turn in for a big collective benefit. When you connect it to your game, the punishment mechanic is less of a threat and more of a way to ensure students complete required work.

Easter Eggs

Explanation

Small secrets that are embedded into the game that most players don't discover

Pros

- Fulfills a sense of curiosity for players who want to explore more of your game world
- The mechanic hits on status, access, and power, depending on how you structure your Easter eggs.
- They create a game lore or mystery for players who pursue them.
- Rewards dedicated game players

Cons

- Sometimes too hard to find; loss of motivation
- Must be special enough to be seen as worth the time investment
- Will not be available to all players

Uses and Ideas

Be ready to embrace that not every component in your game will be used, touched, or experienced by all players. That is okay! Easter eggs are a fun, hidden element that only a few students will experience. Focus your design energies into the challenges of hiding them as well as what students will gain when they discover them.

Mario Brothers, again, provides a great example of this mechanic. In the game environment, there are tubes to jump over in order to reach the goal. Most of them go nowhere, and enemies pop up from several of them. However, and with much excitement, a few do drop you down into a chamber filled with coins. Additionally, when you exit and return to the surface, you are usually farther through the level than when you dropped down—*bonus*!

Students will feel a sense of pride when they find one of these hidden gems. It also builds rapport between you and the students as they feel they share a valuable secret. Easter eggs don't have to be found to win the game; however, they do support other game elements along the way. Additionally, Easter eggs allow us to create reasons to explore our game world and keep students engaged in the game when other parts of the game no longer resonate with them.

Edgar the shopkeeper is the Easter egg in my game, and he is part of every unit. He is hidden somewhere on the class website. Students who find him can spend their gold to buy items from him. It is always fun when we get to a new unit and kids scour the site to find where Edgar is located. They also keep his location secret because of how hard they work to find him.

I also hide quests or course tasks on my site that are not in the normal side quest bank for a unit. Students who frequently explore the course game world find these additional quest options.

Keep in mind that your games can be created with minimal technology. One simple way to hide or reveal an Easter egg is to create the quest or reward in Google Docs. Then create a *bit.ly* or *tinyURL* of the Google Doc link to share with kids who have found the Easter egg. You could put the link in a coded message that students need to crack.

For those who don't feel comfortable using web tools, you can keep the game entirely offline. As students complete different quests, give them an unexpected item or reward that is associated with the task. This could be a paper with additional options that they have access to, now that they completed the quest. An example is the "Daily Double" bonus on Jeopardy.

I also use e-mail inbox rules as the game mechanic. I tell students to email me when they finish a quest, using a particular subject line. The email rule is set up to send the students an email back with instructions for the Easter egg.

Easter eggs definitely drum up excitement for the game, especially when I drop a few hints to students that something is out there. Teams will start to form in order to hunt for these hidden treasures. Anticipation drives the players because they have no idea what the Easter egg will bring.

TRADE

EXPLANATION

Any system that allows players to exchange items or currencies within the game

PROS

- Creates the real feeling of an economy
- Increases the social element of the game
- Works nicely with other mechanics

CONS

- It requires items to trade in order to make this a vibrant element of your game.
- Can be cumbersome to manage

USES AND IDEAS

Trading is essential to making your course game world come alive. Little intervention is needed to add this to your game. I have several items and badges that students earn. Students tape the content badges to their binders, which means they can only be earned and not obtained through trading. Items, on the other hand, are an easily traded element, and students begin to wheel and deal with each other very early on for desired items.

All of this happens without involvement from me. The only rule is that items cannot be traded during class time. This is less about wasting time and more about the fact that trading affects several of my item mechanics. A good example is the level-two spear that allows students to skip a team's turn during reviews. If player one used it, and then traded it with another player in that review session, that player could use it too. This would mean that many students could use that one spear numerous times in one class period. I designed the majority of items in my game for students to use again and again; the only limit is that students can only use the item once each day. Students are taught this rule at the very beginning and follow it throughout.

Game economic systems are a great way to encourage thoughtful game choices. Players must learn to discern wants from needs to continue to be successful and manage their money and items. The trading system also allows students to personalize the game at a micro-level by literally crafting a character in your game. This opportunity taps into their creative and critical thinking skills and gives them a valuable sense of agency.

Through the years, I have added more and more trading elements to my game. I now have ports, where only students with ships can sail and become merchants buying items to bring back to their house, guild, or selves. There is a market that accepts students' gold, but one needs a market badge to shop there. Both the ports and the markets allow interested students to create a sub-economy. By choice, they take on the risk of trading in hopes of earning a profit that can lead to powerful items from the shop. Again, strong communication and critical-thinking skills are necessary in these game components.

FARMING

EXPLANATION

A repetitive low-level task that gives a small, but accumulative rewards and encourages repeated successes

PROS

- Helps level up a player and teaches them how to master certain elements of the game
- Great way to encourage a gamer toward less interesting work
- Rewards mastery and focus

CONS

- Can be dull work
- Often not central to gameplay yet can give a leg up
- Hard to decide a value for these types of tasks—too low and no one will do them, too high and it will again break the game

USES AND IDEAS

Farming, also called grinding or, my personal favorite, treadmilling, can be great in a class game. This mechanic allows you to reward players who complete repetitive classroom tasks. The real challenge is thinking about how to manage and value farming.

In my class, vocabulary work is a farming task. I use graphical flash cards that students have to create with an image on one side and the definition on the other. I use these in class reviews, and they even appear on tests for bonus XP (not bonus grade points).

I also use farming or treadmilling with current events. I allow students to submit a summary of a current event for points. The points increase the more they do. This also works with a class blog or something that requires regular input or attention. The hardest part is determining value, and this will happen through trial and error. Don't worry about getting it just right the first time. Students will know that changes are needed as the game progresses.

Special Challenge

Explanation

A rare, special event (one per month, season, year, etc.)

Pros

- Gives a sense of curiosity and anticipation
- Creates special moments and makes players heroes of the moment, adding excitement and increased status

Cons

- Needs the right balance of rarity to be truly motivational
- Must be worth the trouble to do the challenge

Uses and Ideas

Think Olympics, not unit tests. This is an event that students look forward to the whole quarter—or the whole year. The idea is simple and requires lots of fun fanfare. Just like the Olympics or the World Cup, these types of events create classroom and even grade level community.

In my Greek unit, the Olympic games are epic as is the Mega-Rumble, which happens at the end of each semester. Teams compete in a crazy-huge quiz bowl about world history. I even invite people from past years to help their former houses win. This creates a buzz throughout the whole school. My current students love seeing these former students come to compete and cheer them on.

Overwhelmed by the Cargo? Don't be! As you Navigate the Waters below, remember you can start small. Motivate yourself to try a new mechanic above if you have already gamified. One thing I have learned during my years of teaching a gamified course is that the majority of students are accepting of change; they are adaptable gamers! It won't be long before you hit smooth sailing with your game-based lesson, unit, or course. You will then have the freedom to add, change, and drop game-based elements.

Navigating the Waters: Mechanics

The mechanics of your game tug, raise, and move it in different directions. As Captain, you pull the halyards to hoist the mainsail. You are the one who spins the helm hard to starboard, changing the rudder to alter the ship's course, while the keel helps keep the ship moving straight ahead in the water.

Select *one* mechanic to work on at a time in this section. Decide what you want to add to your game. Then complete Setting the Course. Once you have explored different routes, come back to this list of mechanics and choose another one. Navigate your way through the process again and again as your creativity and game build.

GAME MECHANICS

XP

LEVELS

LEADERBOARDS

GUILD

ONBOARDING

ACHIEVEMENT

QUESTS

EQUIPMENT

SKILLS

POWER UPS

CURRENCY

CASCADING INFORMATION
THEORY

MICRO CHALLENGES &
MINI-GAMES

LIFE JACKETS

PLAYER VS PLAYER (PVP)

COMMUNAL DISCOVERY

TIME EVENTS

PUNISHMENT

EASTER EGGS

TRADE

FARMING

SPECIAL CHALLENGES

SETTING THE COURSE

Pick a route and answer the question(s). Then move to the next section, "Exploring," and further define the details. Start with the route that excites you the most. Come back to the others later.

ROUTE ONE: STORY

Connect the mechanic you have chosen back to your story. What can you name this mechanic?

Examples

- Futuristic skills mechanic: captain, chief medical officer, engineer
- Western currency mechanic: gold nuggets, bullets, livestock

ROUTE TWO: RULES

Rules, rules, and more rules. What rules will help the game take shape?

Examples

- 1,000 points to advance a level
- Must have fire badge before you can work on pottery quests
- Can players trade items or not?

ROUTE THREE: MANAGING

- How will you manage these mechanics in your class?
- XP: Where/when will these points be updated?
- Gold: Will it be physically or digitally tracked?
- Special Event: When does this happen? Is it a surprise or known?

EXPLORING

Now that you have chosen a route, it is time to craft the details. Use the general ideas you created above and spend time exploring possible names, characteristics, and connections. If you get stuck or lose motivation, move on to a new route and come back later with fresh eyes.

EXPLORE ROUTE ONE: STORY

- What language can you create to talk about this mechanic? (e.g., panning for gold, a showdown at high noon, driving the cattle across the open range)
- In what ways will you use this mechanic to drive your story? (e.g., a special challenge, like Olympic events, to earn items in your game)

EXPLORE ROUTE TWO: RULES

- Define the rules of this mechanic in your game.
- Are game points attached to grade points? All the time? Some of the time? Never?
- What is the purpose of this mechanic in your game? How important is it in the overall game? (Many mechanics are fun and cool, but they are not all needed in every game.)
- How will this affect your students/the game? Does this mechanic make the game more challenging? Does it help the struggling students catch up? Does it slow down the lead students? Is this rule important to the structure of the game or is it just to add excitement?
- What are some possible ways you could bend your own rules? (This will help you make items in the next chapter. For example, you could bend the rules through creating an item or badge: no going back to your locker *unless* you have the Off-Base Expedition item/badge.)

EXPLORE ROUTE THREE: MANAGING

- How can you build excitement for this mechanic? (Claiming it's the toughest mechanic, Promoting that the mechanic is coming, Playing music as you introduce a new mechanic)
- Who is in control of this mechanic? Students? Teacher? Team? The game itself?
- Are there classroom activities in which this could be used? (e.g., review games, projects, papers)
- Dynamic duo! What mechanics could play off each other? (Designing a game with XP complements a game designed with Levels.)

Resources

1. Hattrick, http://hattrick.org.

2. Tom Wujec, "Build a Tower, Build a Team," TED.com, February 2010, http://www.ted.com/talks/tom_wujec_build_a_tower.

Tools and Treasure: Stockpiling Items and Earning Badges

A soldier will fight long and hard for a bit of colored ribbon.

—*Napoleon Bonaparte*

ADJUSTING YOUR SAILS

It's time to raise the jib as we take a deeper look at items and badges. Compared to the mainsail, the jib makes minor, but important contributions to propulsion. The jib's most crucial function is as an airfoil to increase performance and overall stability. Items and badges work just like a jib. They will be the airfoil, designed to give the most favorable ratio of lift to your new game. They can serve as mechanisms for corrective feedback as well as motivation to connect with the content at greater depths.

Badges and items are successful when they are created with purpose. They will boost your game in terms of interest, complexity, and flexibility, if they are designed with intention. Students will be drawn into a game that has a mystique and elements they cannot "game" too quickly. A good game is one that has multiple paths to victory. Where a singular path restricts players, allowing for multiple paths encourages players to develop unique solutions through their own combinations and strategies. Students will have opinions about your items and badges and will want to make suggestions. When that happens, the real fun begins because it means students feel ownership both in the game and of their learning.

People often ask me to share or sell my items and badges. I hesitate to do this because, ultimately, they won't work the same for another game or classroom. Badges and items are intimately tied to the game that is unique to the classroom. They incorporate the individual instructor's teaching style, the physical surroundings, and specific connections to course content. In a conversation with author and educator Paul Darvasi, he described gamification as a rare exotic tropical flower. Done right, it should perfectly match the climate and culture of its surroundings. Uprooting that flower and transplanting it into a new environment won't work. The same is true for the elements of your game. You need to cultivate your game and have it intimately connected to your world. When you do that, you will see the true power of gamification.

You need to cultivate your game and have it intimately connected to your world.

Unpacking the Cargo: Items and Badges

With that disclaimer, I have provided a detailed list of items and badges to spark your creativity. They are yours to use and rename to align with your story. We will explore how to assign powers to your items and how students can use them to play off the different mechanics described in the previous chapter. As with the other mechanics of your game, you don't have to have all of your items and badges planned out from the beginning. I am constantly adding new ones as my content unfolds and students give me feedback.

Disclaimer: Avast ye! The following items and badges section is extensive with the purpose of giving you the full breadth of options. Consider it a treasure chest, one to explore in its entirety or one from which to pick and choose as your game unfolds. You will come back to this section multiple times during your playful planning. Go to page 164 for the Navigating the Waters guide to create your plan for incorporating badges and items.

Badges

In my own classroom, I've chosen to use two types of badges: leader badges and mini-badges.

Leader Badges

Each unit has one leader badge that students can earn multiple times. These are earned by going on side quests. These side quests, as previously explained, are all optional and done for enrichment and the thrill of the game.

When students complete side quests and pay specific attention to detail, they earn the unit's leader badge. It is possible that some students will earn several of the leader badges for that unit. In my Egyptian unit, students who excelled in their quests earned a Ramses the Great badge. All badges are taped to their binders for a bit of status and the sense of accomplishment.

Mini-Badges

I use mini-badges on days when I need high participation and student input. They're a great way to give students feedback and are excellent for simulation days because the theme of mini-badges revolves around the activity of the day. I use mini-badges to onboard students who are cautiously waiting on the sidelines as well as to teach game elements and award positive behaviors and choices. As classmates see how and why other students are earning the badges, they are able to better understand the game rules and course expectations.

All badges have a point value associated with them. These points are different from the typical XP or experience points in that they are end-game points, meaning students don't know the badges' values until the end of the game. Keeping their value a secret helps prevent the Jeopardy Effect and keeps anticipation levels high.

The following are examples of in-game powers associated with items and badges. While they won't necessarily work in your game "as-is," they can be tweaked or adapted to fit your theme and story. This cargo is sorted by individual game mechanics. Refer to the previous chapter for a refresher on uses and ideas for game mechanics.

Currency Examples

I use the following currencies to create a rich environment for my yearlong game.

Temples

* **Class:** Mini-Badge

* **More Info:** Artifacts are a type of earned currency. These artifacts have no value, but they can be traded in the unit's temple for special bonuses. The Temple is a badge the students must earn in order to have the privilege of trading different combinations of artifacts for a variety of benefits.

  Students love collecting the artifacts and strategizing when to trade to achieve maximum benefit for themselves or their houses. Having a slew of artifact cards with no value helps when I want to give a student something that doesn't warrant one of the larger game items.

Small Sword

* **Class:** Item

* **Special Power:** adds 20 Battle Points (BP) to the player

* **More Info:** Battle Points are items that students keep in a sheet in their binder. The more items you create, the greater the game options. Some items, like the small sword, only add BP; others have a special power plus BP. I use BP in my review games in several different ways. In the Jeopardy-style review game, teams tally their BP, and this total becomes their beginning score in the game. I have also used BP as a way to buy power benefits, like those listed below, before we play the game.

  - **Second Chance on a Question**—an opportunity to try again on an incorrectly answered question
  - **Item Block**—Other groups can't target them with their items for a round or two.
  - **Safety Net**—can't lose items for next five rounds
  - **Power Runs Points**—Every question after the first that a group gets right is worth double points.
  - **Trample**—If a group gets a question right, they get a private question for themselves. If they can't answer it in the first ten seconds, others can buzz in.
  - **Lucky Leprechaun**—If your group wins, they can find a pot of "gold" at the end of the rumble and earn some items.

BP also helps with breaking ties. The group with the most BP wins!

I use BP as a component during tests. During the Greece test, it is a battle between Persia and Greece. Houses are trying to do the most damage to the enemy. The total of their test points and BP are added together to determine how much damage was inflicted and the degree of success.

FORGE

* **CLASS:** Item/Badge

* **SPECIAL POWER:** can create tools

* **MORE INFO:** The forge is another powerful and coveted reward within the Realm. The forge lets you create items, like the small sword explained above. I list it under currencies as it can create tools. Tools, as a currency, allow students to upgrade some items and badges. These are all activated on a Realm Day.

COMBO POWERS

Combo Powers are the interactions between items and badges that amplify their individual powers.

ICE SWORD + NUBIUS SHIELD + HEAVY ONAGERS

* **CLASS:** Item

* **SPECIAL POWER:** Together, these items makes you unstoppable!

* **MORE INFO:** First, let's take a look at what each one of these items does separately before we look at how they could be used together.

  Ice Sword: Can lock out one number on a dice when rolling. Additionally, it is worth 75 BP. This means on any item that requires a student to roll a die, the student can call out a number that will not hurt them if rolled.

  Nubius Shield: This allows a reroll on all dice rolls in the Realm.

  Heavy Onagers: This item is earned in the last quarter of my game. It is a rather complex item, but realize that students have been playing now for three academic quarters. The Onagers allows a student to deduct points from another house. Students must first roll to "aim." If they roll a one, two, three, or four, they are successful. If they roll a five or six, they don't get to shoot, and their Onager takes damage. The damage is tracked by filling in one circle per damage on the Onager item. There are three circles per Onager item. Once they are all filled in, the item breaks down and gets thrown away. However, if they successfully roll a one through four, they receive six dice. They roll all six dice and for every number six rolled, they do more and more damage to the opposing house.

Example:
ONE SIX = -500 XP DAMAGE

TWO SIXES = -1,200XP

THREE SIXES = -2,100 XP

FOUR SIXES = - 4,000 XP

FIVE SIXES = -6,000 XP

SIX SIXES = -10,000 XP

The Onager is one that students love to earn and try to use, but it typically doesn't do much damage. However, if students have the Ice Sword and Nubius Shield, they are much more likely to earn sixes.

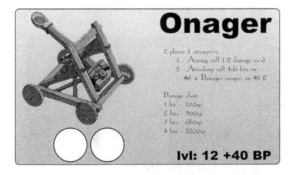

Fire + Fire items

* **Class:** Mini-Badge

* **Special Power:** amplifies other game items

* **More Info:** Students can earn the Fire badge by going on quests or doing phenomenal work in class. This badge can work in combination with several other items. For example, the Neolithic spear is worth five BP (battle points), but if you have the Fire badge, it is worth three times that, or fifteen BP. Students can pair several different items for this combo. This allows the game experience to be customized by the student, providing opportunities for agency.

* **Name:** Hestia's Flame

* **Class:** God Item

* **Special Power:** triples the output of a forge

* **More Info:** Hestia's flame is very powerful; it allows players with a forge to triple production from one forge.

148

LEVELED ITEMS

Leveled items are simple and sound. As you create an item, make a level one, level two, and level three version. With each iteration, the item becomes increasingly rare and powerful. Levels allow for diversity of game options without reinventing the wheel.

SPEAR LEVEL ONE THROUGH THREE

* **CLASS:** Item

* **SPECIAL POWER:** BP and Skip Turn powers

* **MORE INFO:** The spear is designed to be used with my "Royal Rumbles," our class test review days.

    Spear Level One: 20 BP

    Spear Level Two: 35 BP + skip one team's turn once per rumble

    Spear Level Three: 80 BP + skip one team's turn three times per rumble

MERCHANT SHIP

* **CLASS:** Item

* **SPECIAL POWER:** allows players to trade or purchase at restricted shops

* **MORE INFO:** Merchant Ships are a great example of having two powers that are increased by level. In my classroom is a themed island trade port box with all sorts of desired items inside that can only be obtained if a student is willing to risk a merchant ship. On Realm Day (our day for payouts and buying), I announce that anyone with a merchant ship can go to the box and make a trade. Students take out their merchant ship and load it up with items they are willing to risk for a chance at the box. They then roll a dice, and the number will determine if their ship is lost at sea or if they can trade at the box. If lost at sea, the student loses the ship and the items on board. However, if they are successful, they can trade for items at the island trade port.

Merchant Ship Level One: This ship has a cargo hold of one item and rolls two six-sided dice. If you roll above seven, the ship is lost at sea.

Merchant Ship Level Two: Has a cargo hold of two items and is lost at sea by rolling higher than a nine.

Merchant Ship Level Three: Has a cargo hold of three items and is lost at sea by rolling higher than nine twice.

Rule Benders

Rule benders are just plain fun. Students love these because of the fun and strategic ability to break or bend rules in their favor. As your game rules increase, you will start to see ways students can bend rules to benefit gameplay.

Kings Pardon

* **Class:** Item

* **Special Power:** allows you to redo anything in the Realm

* **More Info:** As a kid, one thing I loved about video games was the ability to reload the game to master the level. As a gamified classroom, figuring out just how to structure your redos is the million-dollar question. In my class, "The King's Pardon" allows students to choose to redo something in the course. My standing rule is no redos in the Realm unless you use a rule bender. This has been great because students have put in their best efforts first, as they don't want to have to redo the work as well as use up their King's Pardon. Other students, who know that they will fare well academically, use their pardons on game-related side quests to earn even more points in the game. Being an item, a King's Pardon is something tangible that gives certain students a needed sense of security or safety net. Even if they never end up using it, they feel better knowing they can give any assignment another shot if they want.

Solar Eclipse

* **Class:** Item

* **Special Power:** allows quests to be handed in up to four days late

* **More Info:** One of the rules in my classroom is that side quests have to focus on course content and must be complete by the end of the unit. This item bends the rule and gives students four extra days to hand it in, which has been a huge motivator towards higher-quality quests.

Secret Stash

* **Class:** Item

* **Special Power:** ability to go back to your locker

* **More Info:** Students cannot go back to their lockers once class has begun. This item allows them to break that rule. You could decide to make this an infinite power or a limited one. On mine, I put three small circles at the bottom. When a student uses this ability, they simply shade in one of the circles. Once the three circles are filled, the item is no longer usable. Having circles right on the item puts the onus on the students to track. I have noticed through the years that far fewer students request to go to their lockers now that doing so is a hard-earned ability.

ASSESSMENT

Assessments are foundational to a course and provide an excellent opportunity for items and badges. This is a great opportunity to teach about fairness, as these will affect grades. I explain that everyone has different powers within the game. At first, this may seem unfair, but they soon understand that they all have opportunities to earn these items; the choice is theirs. Earning the powers reinforces the notion that hard work pays off. Students see that those who take the initiative and apply their creativity to a side quest can earn a power that helps them on graded assessments.

STAFF OF WISDOM

* **CLASS:** Item

* **SPECIAL POWER:** 50/50 on one multiple-choice question on all tests the rest of the year

* **MORE INFO:** This is a highly motivating item that honestly makes little difference on an overall test grade. I use it for onboarding, since this helpful item draws in students who may not be fully engaging with the game.

WAR PREPARATIONS

* **CLASS:** House Badge

* **SPECIAL POWER:** gives the class two minutes of open-notes time during a test

* **More Info:** This is a house badge, which means the entire class needs to achieve something in order to make it happen for everyone in the class. An entire class will earn this if everyone scores 85 percent or higher on the online practice quiz. Students become motivated to work together and study hard, which leads to all of them feeling prepared and motivated for test day. Ironically, the two minutes of open notes is rarely needed because the students have studied so much for the practice quiz!

    Because it's a house badge, everyone in the class earns it, which helps boost class morale *and* points at the end of the game.

POTTERY SHARDS

* **Class:** Item

* **Special Power:** Have a note card (cheat sheet) on the test. Sort of…

* **More Info:** During the Greek unit, my largest unit, students are encouraged to earn pottery shards. Each student prepares one note card for the test day that I rip up into six pieces. Each pottery shard they have earned gets them one piece back. Kids love trying to game this system by putting difficult terms and concepts in multiple spots on their note card to ensure they get it back. What I also like about this assessment item is that it is tradeable. If students don't feel they will need the help on the test, they can trade away their shards for items they want. This adds more customization between students and is a win for everyone.

AGENCY-BASED ITEMS AND BADGES

Items, badges, and the powers associated with them give agency to students and their learning. Agency allows students to feel in control of their own game destiny through the belief that their decisions matter. It is almost impossible to feel motivated without agency. Students who don't feel they have agency over their learning often stumble from course to course and project to project with little drive and purpose.

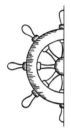

> Items, badges, and the powers associated with them give agency to students and their learning.

The more agency students feels they possess, the better they perform, which leads to more ambitious goals and higher potential for learning. Students with a high sense of agency are more resilient in the face of setbacks and obstacles.

Game-based learning does a great job building in agency because the span of time between making a choice and experiencing the result is instant. That quick result motivates future choices and actions. Games mirror real life in that taking control of our choices leads to a greater sense of control in our lives.

LARGE RAIDING PARTY

* **CLASS:** Item

* **SPECIAL POWER:** doubles the value of a quest up to the value of 750XP

* **MORE INFO:** This item can be used only one time. When a student completes a quest, they decide if they want to use this item or not before I grade it. The ability to make that choice forces them to reflect on their work. They must decide if it is worth using their Large Raiding Party on this quest. In the process, they ask themselves, "Did I do my best? Is this the best time to use this item?"

  This item also helps students catch up, which is another way to give students a sense of agency. If they know that there are ways that they can catch up, they won't ever feel as if they're out of the game.

PHILOSOPHER'S WISDOM

* **CLASS:** Badge

* **SPECIAL POWER:** Create your own side quest.

* **MORE INFO:** I make sure unit side quests run the full gamut, from high-tech to crafty. Even with that variety, my students use their endless imaginations to come up with ideas for things to create, content to explore, and adventures to go on. The Philosopher's Wisdom badge gives them the power to create one side quest per unit. Some are

so good I end up making them into a side quest option for the next year's class.

Making this a badge, and not an item, makes this ability easier to manage. If it was an item, students could create a quest, get scored, and then pass the item on to another member of their guild. By making it a badge, students have to tape it to the front of their binder. This means that only the students with the badge can have the ability to create an additional quest.

Side quests do not earn course extra credit; they earn game points like XP. Students climb over one another to earn this ability to create more work for themselves! You can create emotional need for this item by waiting until the second quarter to introduce it. That way, students have already felt the pain of not liking all the side quests and will be excited to have more agency after the lack of control.

Rollin' the Bones... Dice Modifiers

Dice games are just plain old fun. There is something about playing with dice—the cool anticipation as they roll around in your hand and the fearful hope as you watch your fate tumble across the table. While there are plenty of digital alternatives, I suggest using real dice. A different kind of playful learning happens when we can get off the screen and make it tactile. Dice are easy to understand and generic enough to create all kinds of uses in your game. The items below make great combo powers as well.

LIGHT UTILITY AXE

* **CLASS:** Item

* **SPECIAL POWER:** Roll one through four to earn fifty XP for the day; a roll of a five or six breaks the item.

* **MORE INFO:** Students like this one as they can reuse it each day if they wish, even before class gets started. This helps encourage kids to get to class early. While fifty points aren't that many in my game, they add up over time.

ROMAN SENATOR

* **CLASS:** Item

* **SPECIAL POWER:** add or subtract one pip on a die

* **MORE INFO:** A pip is the dot on the dice. The idea behind the Roman Senator item is that they can change their roll slightly. They can add or subtract one pip on one die. This change can be huge for all sorts of Realm-related tasks. They are only allowed to use this power once a day. They can also use the Senator to help other classmates with their rolls.

THE POWER OF NINE

* **CLASS:** Badge

* **SPECIAL POWER:** The number nine can't hurt you in the game.

* **MORE INFO:** Number nine was the most powerful number in ancient Greece. The Power of Nine adds a bit of lore and legend to the game, as the number nine cannot harm them. It even becomes their lucky number. When nine appears in dice rolling, they can take the action earned with this badge.

TEMPORARY MODIFIERS

Temporary modifiers are based in the Power Up mechanic. The students have limited time to take advantage of the item or spell. Temporary modifiers can be randomly given by you, determined by the dice, or controlled by students' choices.

PERFECT PLUMS

* **CLASS:** Spell

* **SPECIAL POWER:** earns bonus XP if the house doesn't break the spell by talking out of turn

* **MORE INFO:** Students cast spells on their own house or another class house to change game rules temporarily. The

perfect plum spell cast on one's own house requires everyone to be perfect for an entire class period as defined by you. The house successfully earns the XP working together to meet the spell's expectation. The open title of perfect plums allows me to steer the class toward the behaviors and skills they need to work on. For one class, it is about listening to one another; for another class, it is about following directions, and yet another, it is about participation in class discussions.

The Staff of Zwief

* **Class:** Spell

* **Special Power:** curses one player from another house
* **More Info:** This item allows student A to put a "curse" on student B, who is in another house (class section). The cursed player must be a "Perfect Plum" for the whole class period or he or she will lose his or her house's points. The challenge is high because student B and his or her classmates are unaware of who student A picked. It is simply known that someone in this house has been cursed by the staff of Zwief.

Students love to strategize over who to curse. They soon learn that targeting the obvious suspects is not always the best choice as the "good" students are often unsuspecting. They must also work hard at keeping the secret, so the cursed house will lose its points.

Reinforcements

* **Class:** Item

* **Special Power:** During a rumble, earn bonus points for the next three questions your team answers.

* **More Info:** Reinforcements allow a team to earn bonus points on three questions during a class review. At the bottom of this item are three circles, which means that this is a limited item. Students must arrange themselves strategically to provide the best chance at answering the most questions correctly. This item also leads to epic moments in class as teams can come from behind or use them in combination with other items. Students love review rumbles, due much in part to all the player interaction.

Player Interaction

A huge draw in game-based learning is the experience shared by students. Students love collecting and using items that allow them to play off one another. The interaction fostered by this kind of item spices up activities, like review games and simulations.

Jade Statue

* **Class:** Item

* **Special Power:** deflect one item and control whom it now targets

* **MORE INFO:** During a rumble, a group might have a "spear" thrown at them, which means they have to skip their turn. The Jade Statue, used once per rumble, allows one to deflect an attack and even send it on its way to another group. This can discourage attacks in future rumbles, since other groups know using the spear would be futile.

SUMERIAN BOWMAN

* **CLASS:** Item

* **SPECIAL POWER:** pin down two guilds during the next class question—can be used *twice* per rumble

* **MORE INFO:** This one is awesome as it allows the player to prevent two guilds from answering the next class question. Items like these help forge alliances between weaker groups that need to work together to defeat the current leader in the review game.

THIEVES' DAGGER

* **CLASS:** Item

* **SPECIAL POWER:** allows its holder to steal an item from the lost pile after a rumble

* **MORE INFO:** Students might lose items during rumbles if they answer questions wrong. This forms a lost item pile.

Students with Thieves' Daggers have a chance to steal one of those items from me by rolling a die. The number of daggers determines the number you must roll. If you have one dagger, you must roll a one to be successful. If you have two daggers then you can roll a one or a two. Houses work together to stockpile daggers, so that they can retrieve lost powerful items. Some players, who are in it for themselves, work on accumulating daggers as a means of increasing their trading power. Daggers support player interactions and strategical layers.

Navigating the Waters: Items and Badges

Explorers venture into the unknown looking for untold treasure and fame. They risk everything for greater power and glory. Using well-themed items and badges helps harness your students' inner explorers. At the same time, these fun mechanics give players the kind of power and agency that will bring your game world to life and result in endless learning potential.

Using well-themed items and badges helps harness your students' inner explorers.

SETTING THE COURSE

Within this section you will first decide if you are working on an item or badge. You then select a route and brainstorm ideas. Then, depending on whether you are making an item or badge, you move to the "Exploring" section that corresponds to the type of item or badge. Start with the route that excites you the most, and then come back to the others later.

ROUTE ONE: STORY

- Develop a list of possible names for items/badges within the setting of your game world.
- Item examples for a Futuristic theme: disruptor ray, warp core, shield generator
- Badge examples for a Western theme: sheriff's badge, gunslinger, coonskin

> *Caution:* Don't get hung up on what they
> do yet. Simply explore your theme.

ROUTE TWO: COURSE / CONTENT

- Within your content, think of lessons and units that could generate badges/items.
- Item examples for a science class biology unit with a Futuristic theme: electron microscope, laser scalpel, genetic decoder
- Badge examples for an English class poetry unit with a Western theme: cowboy cadence, gold rush rhymes, grammar slinger, haiku herder

ROUTE THREE: GAME

- Are there elements within your game with which items/badges could interact?

Examples

- XP: earn double XP on a side quest
- Rule: can only have one sword
- Item: Sword Rack lets you have unlimited swords

EXPLORING: BADGES

Now that you have chosen a route to create a badge, it is time to craft the details. Use the general ideas you created above and spend time exploring possible names, characteristics, and connections. If you get stuck or lose motivation, move on to a new route and come back later with fresh eyes.

EXPLORING ROUTE ONE: STORY

- Find images that reflect your setting; watch a show or read a book to spark ideas for names of your badges, language you can use to describe their importance/ability, and ways to incorporate them into your story.
- What are the moments within your story that can be enhanced with the influence of badges?

Examples

- Futuristic: receive an additional side quest choice by moving from Lieutenant to Commander
- Western: earn more accuracy in the shootout by moving from Gunslinger to Sharpshooter

- Who are the characters in your story? How can you rank them to offer game status? How can you theme your badges around these characters?

Examples

  - Futuristic: If you can earn the Medic, Security Officer, and Engineer badges, you level up to an Exploration Crew status.
  - Western: Earning Annie Oakley gains you more XP than earning Buffalo Bill.

- How could this badge be earned? Does it attach to your overall story or is it simply a reward?

Exploring Route Two: Course / Content

- What are the moments in your class that deserve badge recognition? (e.g., consecutive days of completed homework, positive participation, leadership in group work)
- What is an activity that students love or hate doing in your course? Think of ways to elevate the task with badge collection/competition.

Examples

  - World History, Map Skills Badge: Master Cartographer earned on map assessments
  - English, Book Report Badge: Thespian earned for an entertaining presentation

- How could this badge be earned by an individual? Small group? Whole class? (e.g., acquiring a certain number/set of items, showing teamwork, everyone in class getting a needed parent's signature)

Exploring Route Three: Game

- Do students earn this badge? Or do students start with this badge and work not to lose it?
- Do badges have a point system attached? Are these points known or unknown to the students?
- Does this badge have any powers attached to it? Does this badge enhance items?
- Are students trying to collect a set? Does the set have even greater value?
- Can this badge be earned multiple times? Does its influence/importance increase the more it is earned?
- Are badges digital or physical?

Exploring: Items

Now that you have chosen a route to create an item, it is time to craft the details. Use the general ideas you created above and spend time exploring possible names, characteristics, and connections. If you get stuck or lose motivation, move on to a new route and come back later with fresh eyes.

Exploring Route One: Story

- Find images that reflect your setting; watch a show or read a book to spark ideas for names of your items, language you can use in describing their power, and possible ways to incorporate them into your story.

- What does this item do in your story? What does it allow students to do that they couldn't before?

  Examples

  - Futuristic: taser that allows characters to stun their enemies in order to escape
  - Western: anti-venom that allows characters to heal from snakebites

- How might the item be earned?

  Examples

  - Futuristic: discovered on an alien planet
  - Western: bartered at the trade depot

- Which characters have the ability to use this item? (e.g., everyone who discovers it, anyone who buys it, the first bandits who steal it, the most powerful wizard who can cast the spell, etc.)

Exploring Route Two: Course / Content

- What is something that students love to do in your course? Are there additional items you could build around these things that allow for greater choice, reward, or control over the game?

- What are things that your students prefer not to do in your course? How can an item add excitement to these undesirable tasks? How might you give students who attained mastery level greater control over these tasks in the future?

  Examples

  - Math: showing their work
  - Band: getting their practice sheet signed
  - Science: turning in lab reports

- Are there repetitive tasks within your course that you could add items around? Examples include reviews, quizzes, class discussions, and team challenges. What power would help a student complete these tasks in an engaging manner?
- Could this item allow for students to control the content covered in class?

   Examples

   - Futuristic: Time Machine allows students to skip ahead or go back to a specific unit
   - Western: Pickaxe allows students to dig deeper into a topic of their choice

- Could this item allow for students to demonstrate learning in a different way? (e.g., creating an oral presentation instead of taking a multiple-choice test, developing a webpage instead of writing a paper)

Exploring Route Three: Game

Managing Items Questions

- Are items physical or digital?
- Do students earn items for the same task?
- Is there a limit to the number of items a student may have at one time?
- Are there class items? Small group items? Individual items?
- What are the pros and cons of letting students trade items?
- How often do the powers of items come into play?

Building Items Questions

- Specifically state the item power. What does this item do? The questions below will give you ideas.
- How rare is the item? Is it available to any student who can earn it, or is there a limited amount?

Examples

  - Futuristic: The first three players to discover a planet receive additional food rations.
  - Western: Any player who reaches the bank receives the reward of five gold pieces.

- Does this item have limited uses? (e.g., one and done, one use per badge level, unlimited use once earned, expires at the end of the unit)
- Does this item enhance other items? Is this item enhanced by other items?
- Are there multiple levels of this item? (e.g., a spear with multiple levels, power increases with each level)
- Is there a requirement for this item?

Examples

  - Futuristic: must pass cadet training before being issued the Standard Defense Taser
  - Western: must have stables before you can get a horse item

- Do you have to collect a certain amount? With a Western theme, for example, once you have collected five pickaxes, you can start your mine.

X Marks the Spot: Finding Joy in Playful Assessment

All truths are easy to understand once they are discovered; the point is to discover them.

—Galileo Galilei

Adjusting Your Sails

Hoist the topsail! It is time to explore the power of mini-games, the principles of side quests, and the fun of outside-the-box assessments. Safe to say, matey, these pages will send you away with pearls of ideas whether you want to design an epic yearlong adventure, a week-long gamified unit, or one dynamite lesson. The topsail is the first to be hoisted and the last to be taken down, which is a perfect analogy for how you can use these pearls throughout your course content. This is another chapter that is overflowing with cargo to unpack and tweak.

As before, the Navigating the Waters section on page 223 will guide you as you look for ways to get better results in your classroom. Make marks, take notes, and let the creative winds continue to direct you toward the New World of possibilities.

Unpacking the Cargo: Mini-Games

Mini-games are the brain breaks in video games. These short segments are fun but don't really fit the overall story. Nintendo's Super Mario Brothers 3 is a classic example of a game with embedded mini-games. One mini-game is a slot machine with the goal of lining up three parts of a sliced up image. If successful, you get the power up of the image. This kind of break from the main storyline provides micro-successes that lead to a temporary confidence boost. They give the player a renewed sense of hope and excitement to continue on with the larger adventure.

Mini-games in the classroom provide the same kinds of "brain break" and confidence builders. They are a fun, unanticipated element of surprise that revives students' interest in the topic and builds a sense of community. The following collection of mini-games includes many of my favorites. The examples work with any subject and are usable in many grade levels. You will find them ideal for a review of course content as well as fun fillers. You will need little to no setup materials, although I do encourage investing in a buzzer system. I recommend the Rolls Game Show Controller or Affordable Buzzers Wireless as good options to get started.

ROYAL RUMBLE

DESIGNER: Michael Matera (@mrmatera)

TIME: one class period

BRIEF: This is a traditional review game with a few twists.

EQUIPMENT NEEDED: various

Optional: You can use Jeopardy-style format with this review game. I like jeopardylabs.com.

SETUP AND FLOW OF PLAY:

Prepare your questions for the review game or make them up on the spot. This game could also work with a Jeopardy-style board.

Set up the classroom by placing a line on the floor where one member from each team will stand. If you have buzzers, use them; if not, go old school. Have students buzz in by touching their heads, knees, toes, or by simply raising their hands above their heads.

Students lose points if they get a wrong answer. This teaches students confidence in the answer, added risk if wrong, and thrill if correct.

At the end of the game, the team with the most points wins. This is a simple game with many offshoots of possibilities!

VARIATIONS: House vs. the Teacher game…

In this version, the teacher earns points for questions that the students cannot answer or get wrong, adding a bit of tension and increasing class unity. Do not provide the answer, as you can use it again in future rounds with different players at the buzzers. Bring the results into the game design by punishing the house for points lost or by giving items for points won by students.

Mystery Box

Designer: Michael Matera (@mrmatera)

Time: one class period / can be done in fifteen to twenty minutes as a review game

Brief: This is a team review game where groups are asked questions. If they get it right, they may choose a "box" to open for points.

Equipment Needed: None

Setup and Flow of Play:

Write the numbers one through twenty-eight on the board and on a sheet of paper. The numbers on the board represent your boxes or briefcases that are filled with points.

On the sheet of paper, write down next to each number what the point value is inside that "box" (see point values below). If you teach multiple sections of the same course, I recommend making several columns of values and putting the class number above the column. This game is so fun that kids will talk about it outside of class. They'll also give away which boxes were worth a lot of points.

Here's a suggestion for dividing up the points in the boxes:

THREE BOXES WITH 50 POINTS EACH

FOUR BOXES WITH 25 POINTS EACH

FOUR BOXES WITH 20 POINTS EACH

FOUR BOXES WITH 15 POINTS EACH

FOUR BOXES WITH 10 POINTS EACH

FOUR BOXES WITH 5 POINTS EACH

FIVE BOXES WITH 0 POINTS EACH

Students work in teams to answer questions. If they answer correctly, they get to choose a box to open. The great thing about this game is anyone can win.

VARIATIONS:

1. Instead of allowing the group to talk through the answer, individuals must take turns.

2. Attach items or powers that bridge to the course game. Here are some examples:

   - Zero the Hero—allows the player to re-pick once when a zero is drawn.

   - The Collector—if a player or group discovers all of one type of point value, that individual or team earns a bonus fifty points.

   - Trap!—Allows a group to write down a number that causes the points to go to their group when someone picks it.

3. Go up to thirty boxes and assign the extra two boxes to earn something special, like something from the list above.

Mega Tic-Tac-Toe

Designer: The world!

Time: ten-minute flash review

Brief: When teams answer questions correctly, they place their shape on a mega tic-tac-toe board.

Equipment Needed: a dry erase / chalkboard

Setup and Flow of Play:

This is a cool twist on the traditional game of tic-tac-toe. Set up nine tic-tac-toe boards in a grid like this:

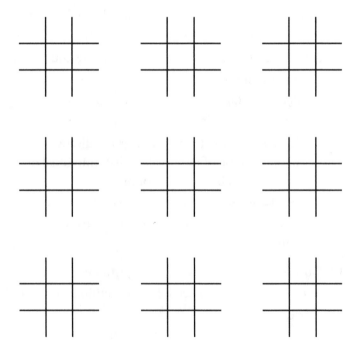

These nine boards now form a kind of large tic-tac-toe board themselves. Begin the game by asking a team a question. If they get it right, they place their first X or O down anywhere on any of the nine boards. However, after the first placement, all others must place marks on the board that corresponds with the individual spot where they put down their last mark. The cell of the board chosen will determine the next board to place their shape when another question is answered correctly. The individual cell is like a map to the overall big board. Example: If the circle team started by placing a circle in the **center** of the top left board, then their next play must take place anywhere on the **center board**. Then, for the next correct answer, they put a circle in the **top left corner** of the center board; their next play will then be back on the **top left board**. Play continues this way until you have a winner.

VARIATIONS:

1. Have more than two teams playing on one board. You could start the triangle team for example! It really throws people for a loop when you have a third team.
2. Make them win on more than one board.
3. Have them try to win boards across the large board forming a line of victories that would win the mega board.

PAPER FOOTBALL

DESIGNER: Michael Matera (@mrmatera)

TIME: one class period

Brief: Students answer questions and then score poker chips. The poker chips allow attempts with paper footballs to score team points.

Equipment Needed:

- Paper footballs (YouTube offers videos on how to make); option to let teams make their own with team color/name
- Poker Chips
- Paper football goal (can be your hands)
- One dry-erase board per team
- Optional use of targets like film canisters, plastic army men, or chess pieces

Setup and Flow of Play:

Divide the class into teams.

Give each group a whiteboard.

Ask the first team a question. All other teams should discuss and write down their answers as well, in case they get to steal the question.

For each question that is answered correctly, the group or player earns a chip.

If the team gets it wrong, the next team can steal the question and earn the points.

At end of class, use five to ten minutes for students to trade in chips for chances to score with a paper football.

Variations:

1. Instead of having them try to score by making a field goal, have them shoot at targets. During my Egypt unit, I placed textbooks all over a table to form a crude map of Egypt, along with little plastic army

men. "Egypt is being invaded" was the scene, and students earned points by shooting their paper footballs at these targets and knocking them down.

2. Give a team an extra shot if they knock over two targets in one shot.

3. Give a team a chance to steal points from another team. First one to knock a canister down gets to take some of the other teams' chips.

GRUDGE BALL

DESIGNER: Kara Wilkins (@kwilkinstchr)

TIME: one class period

BRIEF: In this team-based review game, every team is competing to knock out the other teams and be the last team standing.

EQUIPMENT NEEDED:
- Mini basketball hoop
- Mini basketball

SETUP AND FLOW OF PLAY:

Divide up the class into four to six teams (game will last longer with more teams). On the white board, create a chart showing that each team has ten individual Xs, which serve as the team's life bar.

Each team gets a question. If they get it right, they get to take away two Xs from any one team. The team can choose to take one X from two teams or two Xs from one team.

They are not allowed to take Xs away from their own team. With each correct answer comes a bonus chance: they get to shoot the ball from the two point line or the three point line. If they make it, they then add those points to the total number of Xs taken from other teams. The object is simply to be the last remaining team.

If a team gets knocked out, they still get to play. To get back on the board, they need to answer a question right and make a basket. If they do, they can return with four or five Xs.

VARIATIONS:

Addition of Speed Steal! If the current team answers a question wrong, the other teams have thirty seconds to turn in the correct answer to take away one X from any team.

Addition of a Shielded X! A Shielded X is an X with a circle around it. This is a reward, given by the teacher to any team that has proven themselves worthy— stellar participation in class, winners of last week's review game, most XP points in current classroom game, etc. To remove that X, it takes three points, which put them at an advantage.

If a team becomes the class target, give the team the ability to shoot if they lose more than one X in the next round.

Mini-games are a great place to infuse game items. Create an item that makes the basketball shots worth an additional point or allows a team to take two additional shots.

Mouth of Truth

Designer: Jason Roy (@RoyBot)

Time: one class period

Brief: Teams work together to answer questions and decide whether it is worth pressing their luck with the Mouth of Truth.

Equipment Needed: Crocodile Dentist ($10 Amazon purchase and totally worth it!)

Setup and Flow of Play:

This game is played in phases.

Phase One: Give each team a set of questions to answer. Could be given by PowerPoint, worksheet, or verbally. Teams work through the answers and turn them in to the teacher. Give each team points for the correct answers. The team that got the most right will go first in Phase Two.

Phase Two: Each team sends up one member to press their luck with the Crocodile Dentist. The team with the most points in Phase One goes first; ties go to the team that turned in the answers faster.

The team with the most points pushes a tooth down. If the crocodile's mouth doesn't close, they then choose to continue to push teeth down or lock in the points they earned. The next team continues from where the last team stopped pressing the teeth. The team that causes the crocodile's mouth to close loses their points earned in this phase. Again, students can't lock in until they push at least one tooth.

Tooth / Score
1 / 1
2 / 2
3 / 4
4 / 8
5 / 16

Repeat phases until time is up. Jason also has a third round where the dentist gives out candy. The team with the most overall points at the end gets to play a private round of Phase Two—for candy this time.

Tooth / Candy total
1 / 1
2 / 2
3 / 3
4 / 4
5 / ?
6 / ?

VARIATIONS:

1. During the Phase Two portion, teams lose entire game points if the crocodile's mouth closes. This results in really crazy and wacky scores.

2. Set it up so that each team pushes one tooth down in rounds. Teams can play or pass. Teeth become more valuable with each round. It is hard to walk away. Teams often feel like they have to give it a try.

Danger Cards

Designer: Jason Roy (@RoyBot)

Time: one class period

Brief: This team review game involves high player interaction and bluffing.

Equipment Needed:
- One set of danger cards (make twelve note cards with point values)
- Twelve envelopes

Setup and Flow of Play:
- Start by placing twelve envelopes, each with a card inside, on the board.
- Divide the class into four to seven groups.
- Before play starts, each team gets to peek in one envelope.
- During each round, teams work together to answer three questions. Questions can be given verbally or using PowerPoint. Students write their answers down on a dry-erase board or sheet of paper.
- When done, they turn in their dry-erase board to the answer bin.
- The team with the highest score (by order turned in) chooses an envelope to look inside. They peek and see what it is, and now the bluffing begins.
- All other teams who answered correctly must choose out loud to play or pass, based on reactions of the winning team holding knowledge of the envelope.

- Finally, the original winning team now chooses to play or pass, based on the envelope, and points are then added or subtracted from them, and other teams, accordingly.

- Each team gets one Z chip (can be any kind of marker) to undo one play or pass decision.

- Highest score wins!

Example Setup

ENVELOPES					CARDS INSIDE ENVELOPES			

ENVELOPES			
☠ 1	☠ 2	☠ 3	☠ 4
☠ 5	☠ 6	☠ 7	☠ 8
☠ 9	☠ 10	☠ 11	☠ 12

CARDS INSIDE ENVELOPES			
-100 pts	-25 pts	-50 pts	-50 pts
Steal Another Teams Pts Rvs Ord	25 pts —+— Peek	25 pts —+— Peek	50 pts —+— Peek
Swap Pts. w/Team Rvs Ord	Lose Double Your Pts.	Lose all your pts.	100 pts —+— Treasure

The cards that have a + something at the bottom are only meant for the team that chooses the card.

VARIATIONS:

This mini-game works in any subject. Jason is a high school math teacher, and he uses it to have students solve three hard math problems. I use it to answer three world history questions.

1. Play around with the point totals and special powers.

2. Attach game elements, like items and XP, to the course.

Gator Golf

Designer: Jason Roy (@RoyBot)

Time: one class period

Brief: Teams answer questions and earn poker chips. At the end of the game, the poker chips turn into opportunities to score points through golf putting.

Equipment Needed:
- Putter
- Golf balls
- Putting green or ball return
- Poker chips or golf tees
- Dry-erase boards for each group
- Optional: Mini golf club pencils to take notes

Setup and Flow of Play:

This game is played in three rounds. However, if you finish only one or two rounds, it still works.

Form teams.

Round One: Ask sixteen questions, one question at a time. All groups answer on dry-erase boards.

Teams take turns answering questions. Teams earn a tee (or poker chip) when they answer correctly. If the team answers incorrectly, the next team gets a chance to answer and earn a tee. Turns switch with each new question.

Bonus: Golf Round! Tally the tees to determine the point score. The team with the most points gets to putt closest, but not too close, to the hole. Other groups shoot farther and farther back. Everyone on the team gets a shot. Hit the hole and earn one point; make the putt and earn three points. You should be able to do this in seven to eight minutes. If you want it to go faster, have half of the members on a team putt.

Round Two: Using PowerPoint or other media, offer several, longer-form questions. In reverse point order, have teams select a question to answer. If a team finishes early, they can try to work on the other teams' questions to prepare to "steal" the question from a team that answers incorrectly.

Golf Round: One putt per right answer, so this golf round goes quickly.

Final Round (Optional): Wager points on one final putt. Highest total wins!

VARIATIONS:

1. Just continue to play Round One until you only have ten minutes left in class. Each correct answer a team gives earns them one putt in the final score round. The bonus to this method is you get to ask more questions and don't have to set up ahead of time.

2. If using poker chips, have questions worth different values and, thus, different chip colors. Example:

   Blue = double putt

   Green = start much closer to the hole

   Red = attack another group by placing an obstacle

   White = group with the most white gets to choose putting order of all teams

   Black = double value if you make the putt

3. Only score points for sunken putts.

Treasure Hunter

Designer: Philip Vinogradov (@pvinogradov)

Time: five to ten minutes

Brief: This is an activity for students to collaborate over answers to large essential questions or unknowns.

Equipment Needed: Dice (four per group)

Setup and Flow of Play:

Start with a meaty question, something that causes discussion and multiple answers.

Have each group roll the four dice together. The groups now try to discuss and answer the question by using the exact amount of words as the sum of their dice. This gives groups a range of four to twenty-four words.

Give students a few minutes to discuss and formulate an answer. Then each group shares their response. Students love to hear what each group did with their words, especially when one group only had seven while another had nineteen, for example.

Variations:

Philip also uses this idea to brainstorm words and concepts associated with the topic. All teams roll the dice and then write numbered word responses in columns on the same Google Doc. The Google Doc shows both the thinking that took place as well as the result.

Post-it Pause

Designer: Philip Vinogradov (@pvinogradov)

Time: five to ten minutes

Brief: This mini-game is an in-class question technique that keeps students listening, thinking, and working in teams.

Equipment Needed:
- Post-it notes (This is a must; do not do this one digitally.)
- Dice (one per group)

Setup and Flow of Play:
Give each group a few post-it notes.
- *Step One:* Start your regular lesson for the day. After you have covered a portion of the content, go to Step Two.
- *Step Two:* Reflect
  You will now give students a post-it pause to reflect on the lesson. Give them time to write down any questions about the lesson. After giving students two to five minutes to reflect, continue with the regular lesson. At about the halfway point of class, move to Step Three.
- *Step Three:* Group needs assessment
  Have the teams share their lesson questions with one another. Tell them to rank the questions in order of importance. As a team, they work together to answer the questions they confidently know. Then they form the list of questions that are still unanswered, ranking them in order of importance.

- *Step Four:* Roll for response
Each team rolls, and the team with the highest number rolled gets to ask their question. All ties result in a roll off. The team asks their question and receives their answer. I tend to do about three of these before repeating the entire cycle again.

(REPEAT CYCLE AGAIN) Students can still ask questions from Round One.

One of the things I love about this activity is that, because each individual student reflects and writes, every player has skin in the game. When groups get together, it is fascinating to see how they are lobbying for their questions. Philip says, "It is like they wrote it in their own blood." Once the roll off happens and a group gets to ask their question, the amount of active listening is impressive. Each group pays attention to hear which questions they can take off their lists, as I answer questions. When you go back in the roll off, there's a ton of excitement and anticipation as one group member holds the lifeblood of your question in their hands. Inevitably, fate takes over and hope rises and falls with the settling of each die. Collectively, the energy in the room has been transformed through this simple game.

Variations:

I like to spin this with my gamified class to see if other tables can answer their classmates' questions. If it is a well-articulated full answer, their team will earn a choice of +1 on their next roll or reroll.

SHUFFLEBOARD SURMISE

DESIGNER: Erica Czerniki (@MsCzerniki)

TIME: one class period

BRIEF: Students work in teams to compete for poker chips that they will later use to score shuffleboard points.

EQUIPMENT NEEDED:
- Poker chips
- Butcher paper for tables
- Butcher paper for shuffleboard
- Shuffleboard discs and cue
- Questions on PowerPoint

SETUP AND FLOW OF PLAY:
Break the class into teams. Each team gets a sheet of butcher paper to post answers.

Start by asking the students a question. Teams work together to write or draw their answer to the question. When completed, the teacher (as the judge) assesses the answers with the following criteria.

Poker Chip Rubric:
- One chip = Right answer but not cool
- Two chips = Right answer + creative and full response
- Three chips = Right answer + you blew my mind

You keep repeating rounds like this until you run out of questions or only have eight to ten minutes left in class.

At the end of the class, have each group play shuffleboard.

You take your created sheet and place it on a table or the ground. Each team uses all their disks to score as many points as possible. Feel free to experiment with different shuffleboard setups. Erica's original board had point values that ranged from 1,000 to 2,000 and even had the back work -1,000 points. The team with the highest total wins.

VARIATIONS:

1. Use this as a test review with a twist. Have students make notecards for the test. Cut each notecard into four pieces. Then as they play the game, they must compete to earn back their notecards for the test. Scoring 1,000 pts = one part of the card back to use on the test.

2. Have students be the judges of the answers. You can still act as the master judge, so if they don't do a good job, you take points away from their team. However, if they do a fair and good job, they can earn points for their team.

3. Have all teams play on the same shuffleboard, taking turns with shots. This way, they can knock teams off the board. *Ouch!* With this style of play, you could get your game designer hat on and start thinking of crazy rules to add. For example, some of the chips they earn in the question rounds would be special chips.

   Examples
   - Blue chips allow the team/player to shoot and score, then remove their disc so no one bumps it.
   - Red chips score a highest value within a disk range.
   - Earn three green chips to turn all negative points on the board to positive for your team.

Build Challenge

Designer: Michael Matera (@mrmatera)

Time: one period, could be less

Brief: reading summary

Equipment Needed:

- LEGO bricks—I use LEGO Bricks & More Builders of Tomorrow. I provide one set per team so they all have the same materials.
- LEGO mini-figurines
- Kapla Blocks (optional for game variations)

Setup and Flow of Play:

This activity is a build challenge for my guilds within each class. After we have covered a chunk of content, groups use the LEGO bricks to build three key moments of history.

I intentionally want to make this group challenge a difficult one. The students have forty minutes to build three scenes, take photos, and then write a summary of each scene. The photos are loaded into iMovie, and the students must create a voiceover for their pictures. You only need one recording device per guild, and you can utilize a smartphone, tablet, or laptop. This mini-game supports strong team building and communication skills as students have to create a plan and manage their time well in order to succeed.

Variations:

1. Use a bell or gong. When teacher sounds the bell or gong, students must continue working together without talking.

2. Cage Match—Create an additional guild just for that day. To populate this new guild, tell the existing guilds that they must pick a team captain for the day's activity. Before starting the LEGO-building activity, call up the captains and explain that they, for today only, form the new guild. Then construct a cage. I lean four folding tables together. Instruct the newly formed guild to enter the cage. The students in the cage use Kapla blocks, similar to Jenga blocks, which are harder to construct scenes with than LEGO bricks. Move forward with the game.

Graffiti

Designer: Michael Matera (@mrmatera)

Time: twenty-five minutes

Brief: a funky preview activity

Equipment Needed:

- Classroom board (chalk or dry erase)
- Several writing tools
- Music!

Setup and Flow of Play:

Use this as a preview unit. Instruct students to look at the pages of the new chapter and find key terms, important concepts, and specific details. For my history class, that could mean looking at a map page in the chapter and pulling out some of the rivers, mountains, and city names, or it could be key people, inventions, and beliefs of a culture.

When students find a term or concept, they raise their hand and, when called upon, race to the board and write it for all to see. Then they return to their seat and repeat as fast as they can. They are trying to populate the board with a mountain of information. Play music in the background that will motivate them to work quickly. It is intense! Sometimes, I call up a whole wave of students to the board. If you have XP for your game, you could insert it in this activity and say that you will give some XP to those players who have a tenacity and zeal at finding and writing unique terms on the board.

When time is almost up, I play the song "Under Pressure" by Queen as the warning signal they only have a couple more minutes. When done, I have a powerful visual of all the information and work that lays ahead for the guilds and houses. I give a brief motivational speech that it will take a lot of hard work, focus, and perseverance to learn and understand all this information. I tell the students that the learning doesn't begin the night before the test or only on their papers or projects. The learning begins today; the learning begins *now*!

At the end of the game, I take a photo of the board in order to count the unique words they earned. I will admit it is not a perfect science; I scan them, counting up the words I can see and read that are unique. I do this for each of my classes and the class that got the most unique words wins!

Quick Rules

- To avoid repeats, instruct students to look at what others are putting on the board.
- Instruct them to write small, so many words can fit on the board. One word is only worth one point; it's not about size.
- Students start when the music begins to play. They stop when the music stops.
- What they write must be important information from the chapter.
- They must raise their hand and be called on before running to the board. They can only write one word or concept at one time. Then they sit back down and repeat until time runs out.

VARIATIONS:

Later in the year, I like to get a bit crazy and introduce the idea that if students touch an unused chair, they have to sit in it as a timeout until I set them free. For example, I will grab a few extra chairs and call students up to the classroom board. While they are writing, I will place a chair right behind them. Friends will be screaming for them to stay still, but they usually end up bumping the chair. It really makes this game super fun for all and makes the class work together.

WAGER ON WISDOM

DESIGNER: Michael Matera (@mrmatera)

TIME: one class period

BRIEF: a review game

EQUIPMENT NEEDED: poker chips

SETUP AND FLOW OF PLAY:

Give each team enough chips to equal 100 points.

Set up an inner half circle of chairs and an outer half circle of chairs that arch behind the team's individual answer chair.

One team member starts in the answer chair.

Rules:

1. All answer-chair players are on their own.
   - No turning around
   - No communication with their team
2. All answer-chair players must write down their answers to all questions.
3. The other team members are called the Wager Members. These players must wager on the player who answered the question. If the team gets the right answer, the pay is 3:1. Bonus: If the answer-chair player gets it right as well, the team earns 5:1. However, if their player gets it wrong, it only pays out 2:1.

This is a fun review game where students really have to practice active listening and work together to earn the most points possible. To keep it flowing, I have a student pay out the amounts owed and have had very few problems.

VARIATIONS:

An additional setup item is a wager board that you create for each team. In this game, the wager members need to choose where to place their wager. Boxes on the board can include any combination of the following:

- No one is right = 5:1 payout to the individual that knows the answer

- Only my team is right = 4:1 payout

- All players are right = 3:1 payout

- Have a box with all the group names; students can wager on which group will have it right; winners get 2:1 payout.

- Your team has it right + a group box above + one payout per group; must have all groups that you bet on right.

- Let it ride: This zone is broken down into three zones. Zone One: two questions; Zone Two: three questions; and Zone Three: four questions. If a team gets that many right in a row, they earn 3:1, 4:1, 5:1 payout respectively.

Vocab Taboo

Designer: A spinoff from the Hasbro game

Time: five minutes to an hour

Brief: Create Taboo-style vocab cards for a fun assignment. Once you have enough cards, you could use them as a review game with students.

Equipment Needed: Students or teacher make Taboo cards related to course content.

Setup and Flow of Play:

Taboo is a board game from years back. This game requires students to think about vocab from a bit of a different angle. Players must draw a card and, through hints, get their partner or team to say the word at the top of the card. The hints cannot include the five words listed below the top word on the card. In our version of the game, students create these cards with their vocab words, which engages their critical thinking skills about the content.

Example

Kangaroo
POUCH
HOP
ANIMAL
AUSTRALIA
CAPTAIN

Students really have enjoyed this as a side quest option, homework, or in-class activity. I have used this for a Royal Rumble as well, and the kids really enjoyed playing. I find it particularly useful when you are prepping for something really big, like a mid-term exam; that way, students don't know which specific unit the vocab term is coming from.

Unpacking the Cargo: Fun Fillers, Brain Breaks, and Team Building

Fun fillers are just that—an activity for the end of a lesson when you only have five minutes left or need a bit of a brain break. They work in multiple grade levels and are especially ideal for middle schoolers.

Super Silent

Designer: Michael Matera (@mrmatera)

Time: one or two minutes

Brief: Students have to harness their inner ninja in order to complete tasks silently.

Equipment Needed: none

Description and Flow of Play:

Students must complete whatever challenge you decide without making a single noise. This game, while silly and fun, builds teamwork.

Tell the students that they need to harness their inner Navy SEAL. They need to control every last muscle in their body. If you hear a knee crack or a bracelet clink, they will have to start the level over again. The first level I always start with is having students all sit in their seats and just trying to stand up. Simple enough? It usually takes them three or four attempts to achieve this level. It is important that you really are a hard judge during this level, as you want to set the bar high. After they complete this level, I give them another challenge to do.

Sample Levels

1. Start seated and stand up.
2. Start standing and try to sit and then hold still for thirty seconds.
3. Start with chairs pushed in and students standing. They need to pull out the chair and sit down.
4. Sit on the ground, then pair up with a partner and try to stand up by leaning back to back with partner.
5. Start on their bellies and attempt to stand up.
6. Switch seats with someone on the opposite side of the room.
7. Close their binders and hold for thirty seconds.
8. Stand on one leg for fifteen seconds.
9. Touch their heads, shoulders, knees, and toes.
10. Start standing, sit, hold for thirty seconds, then stand up on cue and hold for thirty seconds.

COUNT DOWN

DESIGNER: unknown

TIME: five minutes

BRIEF: Students pick a number with the goal of picking the lowest number without anyone else picking the same number.

EQUIPMENT NEEDED: none

DESCRIPTION AND FLOW OF PLAY:
This game is quick and addictive. To start, everyone

thinks of a number and writes it down. Once everyone has selected a number, the teacher calls out numbers in descending order. If students picked that number, they call it out. If they are the only one that picked that number, then they are the current front-runner. If more than one person chooses the same number, then all of them are out. You then call the next lower number; if a single person picked that number, you have a new front-runner and the old one is out. If two or more people picked that lower number, then they are out, the former front-runner remains in the lead, and you call the next number. You keep calling numbers until no one is left.

POISON

DESIGNER: unknown

TIME: eight minutes

BRIEF: similar to hot potato

EQUIPMENT NEEDED: none

DESCRIPTION AND FLOW OF PLAY:

Choose a top number.

Tell the students the target number is ten, for example.

Each student on his or her turn can say the next number in order or the two next numbers. For example, the first player says one and two, second player says three, and third player says four and five. It keeps going around like this until someone has to say ten. Once that happens, that person is out and the counting resets. The goal is to be the last player standing.

Beanbag Toss

Designer: Michael Matera (@mrmatera)

Time: ten minutes

Brief: The game is a cross between Super Silent and Simon Says with beanbags.

Equipment Needed: small, hand-sized beanbags

Description and Flow of Play:
Pick a spot to stand:
1.   Stay in the spot with little movement.
2.   No talking!
3.   Toss beanbag underhanded.
4.   Make good tosses and catches.
5.   You can't get out from someone who is out.
6.   Pay attention to the additional rules that get added.

Let's break these rules down:
Rule one: Stay in your spot. This is simply to ensure they are not diving to catch the toss and are not running around to avoid catching. They must pick a spot and stick to it.

Rule two: No talking. If a player breaks this rule, he or she is out of the game.

Rules three & four: Toss underhanded and make good tosses and catches. This is just so the students get the point that it is not about making a fast toss. The goal is to make good tosses and good catches. They need to remain in the game. Nothing more.

Rule five: You can't get out from someone who is out. If a student drops the catch, she is now out, but the beanbag is right at her feet. She then picks it up and tosses it quickly to anyone else. If the receiver drops it, he is not out because the thrower simply brought the beanbag back into play.

Rule six: Pay attention to the additional rules. This is the crux of the game. Add additional rules like "catch with your left hand" or "use only two pinkies." If they don't, they are out.

Play until only one person is left, or add the following as an option:

When you're down to six players, ask three to sit on the floor on one side of a table and three to sit on the other side. In this round, there are four new rules added:

Rule one: Throw overhand. They can throw overhand (not for speed, but to make it easier since they are throwing over and under the table).

Rule two: The teacher can throw to someone and get them out. Toss the beanbag; if they don't catch it, they are out. Additionally, if this round is taking too long, bring in a second beanbag to add more challenge about where to look.

Rule three: You must make a clean toss. The toss can't hit anything above or below the table, such as a book or chair; if it does, the person who tossed is out.

Add chairs and other objects above or below the table, which invites additional rule possibilities. When down to final two students, have them stand and face each other. Go back to the standard rules, including that the teacher can toss as well. Invite other students to walk at a consistent pace back and forth, requiring the players to avoid hitting them.

Bubble Wrap Tournament

Designer: Michael Matera (@mrmatera)

Time: one minute per game

Brief: Two students face off and pop bubble wrap!

Equipment Needed: bubble wrap

Description and Flow of Play:

Two students face each other while kneeling on three-by-three-inch squares of bubble wrap. After you shout go, the students must grab the bubble wrap from under their own knees and bring it behind their backs. They now start popping it as fast as they can. When one feels they have popped all the bubbles, they shout, "Done!" and hold up their bubble wrap. You then inspect and see if there is even a single un-popped bubble. If so, they lose, and the other player—no matter how many bubbles they have left—wins. This works very well in a tournament style. Let it last for several days and then declare the winner.

Penny Drop

Designer: Every kid in the world!

Time: one second

Brief: Put a small target in the bottom of a deep container of water. Students have one penny to drop with the goal of getting it to land on the target.

Equipment Needed:
- Small target (I use a shot glass.)
- Deep glass container (wide-mouth pitcher, fish bowl, or dish tub, for example)
- Pennies (at least # per student)

Description and Flow of Play:
The game is a simple penny drop. Due to the water, it is really hard to get that penny to land on the target. This game can be a chance reward, meaning that if a student hits the target with his penny, you hand over a reward item. If you are gamifying your course or unit, this can be a fun random addition to your game. Players can buy or earn some chances to do the drop and, if they're successful, they earn a game item.

Bobsled Challenge

Designer: Michael Matera @mrmatera

Time: Three minutes

Brief: Divide class into two teams, then have them line up their chairs into two straight lines. These are their bobsleds.

Equipment Needed: Chairs set up in two parallel lines to form competing bobsleds

Description and Flow of Play:

Students start by standing outside their chair sled on alternating sides, like in the Olympics. When you say go, both teams start by pretend-pushing their chair sleds while running in place. Then shout, "Jump in!" Just like a real bobsled race, they need to file in front to back. The faster and smoother they make this transition, the better. Then shout directions to lean left, straight, right, hard left, or hard right. Students must follow those directions as a team. After a bit of fun, decide who had a cleaner race and deem them the winner. Students love this easy and simple team-building game. If anyone falls out of a chair, it is automatic disqualification for the team. You can add hard challenges, like switching sleds or turning chairs around. This always throws them for a loop.

UNPACKING THE CARGO:
BEYOND THE BUBBLE—PLAYFUL ASSESSMENT

The following are ideas that fall outside the usual norms of assessments. As with many elements outlined in this book, students have found these to be motivating because they are both a challenging and creatively different way to find out what they know.

DOMINOS

This idea is from my good friend and colleague, Chuck Taft (@chucktaft). It involves creative processing and critical thinking. Take important topics from your content and place them on a domino template, using words or images.

Individually or in groups, students must match up what goes together and then write an explanation for the connection. The goal is to provide thoughtful answers while not getting trapped with too many dominos that don't link together. Blank sides are also an option and require additional thought to successfully connect to other ones.

Odd One Out

Odd One Out comes from the old *Sesame Street* segments with Big Bird called "One of These Things is Not Like the Other." This question uses higher-order thinking. Students must fill in the answer box by defining the three components that fit together, along with reasons for why the fourth does not. These work well for tests. Here's an example from my classroom:

The Shiji	
Mandate of Heaven	
Analects	
Art of War	

Sketch Pad

Pictured on the next page is a test question that asks students to draw the definition of the Acropolis from both the top and the side view. This style of question is open to interpretation. However, with something like Acropolis, there are key things that need to be in the image, such as a high hill. These test items can also be used to connect an image to an idea, like democracy or math fractions. Thinking visually about a vocabulary term or idea can really push students to go well beyond the surface level of the content.

Below draw an acropolis from a top down view & a side view. You may label the drawing if you think it will help.

Top down view   /8   Side View

VARIATION:

The following visual test item asks students to draw and write out their essay on three storyboard panels. They must draw an image and use two vocabulary terms in their answer. This is a great method to show cause and effect and works very well for story arches.

LEGO Build

Give each student a bag filled with building materials (a mix of LEGO and Kapla blocks). A page of their test is a large box titled "Build Zone." The test directions instruct students to build three scenes from their unit; when competed, they take a photograph of what they built. They then place that photo in a Word or Google document and write a brief description (one to three sentences) to explain the significance of what they built. They then disassemble and repeat the exercise for two additional scenes.

A variation of this test activity is to place a small box inside one medium box, which is inside one large box. Students have to build three scenes, one inside each of the different-size boxes. This is more challenging and requires students to map out their answers, think about which ones will need more or less space, and build accordingly.

RORY'S STORY CUBES

Rory's Story Cubes can be purchased on Amazon or at major retailers, including bookstores and toy stores. They include a set of nine dice, all of which have different images on each side. This produces over one million different picture combinations. Students roll the nine dice, take a photo of their roll, and then write about how the images relate to the lesson. The activity challenges students' knowledge and creativity, as the images have very little to do with the course curriculum.

Actual 6th Grade Student Example

Evil Monster Thing: Legalism was a belief that people are bad by nature and need to be controlled. Lots of people did not like it, but the people who did were called Legalists.

GROUP TESTS

Group testing is a simple concept, but one that I think needs a shout out sometimes. Students go deeper into the content when they work together, craft their answers, and discuss questions and understandings. I have been amazed each time at how much evidence of learning students show with these assessments.

Boss Battles

A Boss Battle is more of an idea than a finished way of doing something for an assessment. Give each player three poker chips to represent their health points in this battle. They will be working as a whole class to defeat a fictional "boss." (In my class, one of the original bosses was Squareganom). You start by asking the entire class the first test question. Call on a random student for an answer; if they get it wrong, they lose a health point. Their guild can also choose to try to answer the question. If the guild gets the answer wrong, they all lose a health point.

If a student or guild gets the question right, they then get to roll a die. This die determines the amount of damage they do to the boss. Bosses have a set amount of health points before they are defeated.

You can add additional rules to the game. One example could be that in order to do damage to the boss, a player from each guild must get a question right. The same rules as above apply; if one or more gets it wrong, everyone takes damage.

Unpacking the Cargo: Side Quests

A side quest is an *optional* activity or project within the game that can help unlock or earn game items. The opposite of a side quest is a required assignment that students must perform in order to complete the course. This is a key distinction. I make side quests a big part of my yearlong game because they encourage students to become voracious learners and courageous explorers. Side quests are a great place for students to experiment with new techniques, learn from failure, and innovate without fear of losing grade points.

The first rule of thumb is to allow side quests to be very open ended; they become extraordinary when students drive the creativity of the project. Students can choose from quick quests that are open for a limited time or from the ever-challenging pickup quests that require group work. Whatever the style, remember one simple rule: Side quests are not traditional assignments.

An important learning opportunity provided by side quests is that students become less dependent on their teacher for initiative and content acquisition. In seizing the opportunity, they discover how capable they are of taking risks and determining their own limits.

One way to support this open-ended feel is to keep the side quest directions very short and open to interpretation. I mentioned earlier that the following simple rules guide my students for every unit side quest:

1. You can only turn in your side quest once, so do your very best!
2. The side quest must connect to the current unit.
3. The side quest must be turned in before the unit test.

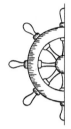

In seizing the opportunity, students discover how capable they are of taking risks and determining their own limits.

These three simple rules help manage the assessment of side quests. I encourage students to do their best work because, just as side quests aren't required for them, they aren't required for me. I want them to understand that, if I am going to take extra time assessing their side quest, their work needs to be extraordinary. I realize, however, that by not allowing redos on side quests, I am losing out on one of the best aspects of gamification, which is the ability to learn from failure and try again. For this reason, I created multiple opportunities for students to earn redos through power ups, items, and spells. They are rare, but they are available to those who earn them. This strikes a balance, which dissuades students from mediocrity and pushes them to become the best versions of themselves.

The second rule, "Your quest must always pertain to the current unit," provides greater ease of implementation; I don't have to write directions that include specifics about the chapter or topic. A great example of brevity of directions is on my map side quest. The directions simply state, "Make a map!" What I love about this style of directions is that different students can take this simple direction and end up in very different places. I have had students hand draw a map of a city while others search YouTube for a salt relief map and end up making a 3D terrain map with hundreds of toothpick labels. A golden interaction happens between students as they learn from one another about how they tackled the challenge differently and give one another feedback on the outcome.

The third standing side quest rule is that the project must be turned in by the end of the unit assessment. Students soon realize that side quests reinforce the content from the unit, which helps them on their assessments. The rule also motivates them to get started early; they know once the unit is over, those quest options go away. I post the side quest options on our class's website, and students choose which they want to complete based on their interests.

In the spirit of game-based learning, these side quest rules of course have work-arounds that students can earn. Remember, with each rule should come a way to break that rule. Once you get started, it will become easier to start thinking of items and power ups that work in combination with your side quests.

Here are some simple examples of side quests for you to customize or use as springboards of ideas for your own side quests.

Clay Creation

For this quest, you must create something inspired by the current unit with clay.

Busta Rhyme

Write a poem; any style is okay. Whatever you do, get creative with the content.

Double Take

Compare the similarities of the temples of Mesopotamia to the temples of the Americas. You determine what to create to compare these two. Be creative in the way you display the information.

49 Cents of Fame

Design/Create a commemorative stamp honoring people, depicting elements from the period, and/or using challenging vocabulary terms.

Copy Cat

Create the cover of a major magazine. It must feature a realistic-sounding article title about our current unit. *Your job is not to write the article.* Your job is to make a very realistic magazine cover, so people believe it is real. Pay attention to every detail.

Family Tree

Create a family tree for the current unit.

Music Man

Write new lyrics to the tune of an old television theme song (such as *Brady Bunch*, *Gilligan's Island*, or *Flintstones*) using an event or topic from the current unit. The better the info, the better the project.

Building to the Sky

For this quest, you *and your house* must build a replica of the pyramids found on MinecraftEDU.

Cartographer's Masterpiece

Create a map of something in our current unit.

Civil Engineer

Construct a model of the city of Rome using any method you see fit. Make sure you include the important landmarks!

You Are There

Recreate the old *You Are There* broadcast series. Make sure to add sound effects and have several characters.

Infographic

Create an infographic about something in the current unit. Do a Google search for "infographic" to get an idea of what one looks like.

Google Doodle

Create a Google Doodle drawing. You must include a paragraph of information describing the item, event, or person from the current unit. Also, include the date that this will be up on Google.

Roman Rap

Create a song or rap, or any other style of music, and record it! Must include information from the current unit and show mastery of the material.

Ignite Speech

Create an Ignite-style speech (five minutes, twenty slides). One tip: practice, practice, practice!

Can You Read Me Now? —Instant Message (IM) Conversation

Write out an instant message conversation between two characters from the current unit.

Postcard

Create a postcard that you would send home from one of the main events, characters, or ideas in this chapter. For this quest, you must write from the perspective of someone in the story.

Words of Wisdom

Write a letter to someone in our unit giving them advice on how to deal with a hard situation in which they find themselves.

Report Card

Create a fake report card for something in the unit. The report card for this "student" could be anything. Make your "student" a character from history, a famous math principle, or a type of organ in the body. No matter what, think outside the box and fill in their report card.

Bumper Bling

Create a visually good-looking bumper sticker that includes a catchy slogan.

Common Craft Video

With a team, work to construct your very own video on a topic of interest in this unit.

Wanted Poster

Take anything from this unit (seriously, you don't have to limit yourself to a person) and create a Western-style "wanted" poster from the Wild West.

Click, Click, Click—Stop Animation

Make a stop animation scene that explains a concept in the unit. You don't have to use LEGO bricks; but I would, because I love them.

Baseball Card Series

Create a series of baseball-style cards for several historical figures in this unit. Take time to make it look like they all come from the same company. Think of statistics that someone from the era might use to rate the historical figures from this unit.

Fast Flash

You have twenty-four hours to turn in a set of at least five flashcards. On one side, draw a picture to represent the vocabulary word; on the other side, write the word and its definition.

Mix Master

First, select an important passage from our text or something you researched. Second, use an audio editor, like GarageBand, to record yourself reading the passage. After that, lay down some beats and loops to create an audio masterpiece.

Six-Word Challenge

This is a fast quest; you have until next class to complete a six-word challenge. *(I got the idea of these from* Smith Magazine's *six-word memoirs. These are quick challenges where students have to try to summarize a whole chapter or unit in just six words. It is fun to see all the creative word play.)*

Curator of Curiosity

You need to make a new exhibit that will be on display at our local museum. The only catch is that the museum needs a bit of convincing. For this quest, you need to make the exhibit and write up a marketing pitch promoting why this exhibit should join their permanent collection.

These side quest examples show short and direct instructions that still leave room for students' interpretation and creativity, which is the magic formula for side quests.

As with all the chapters in Setting Sail, this is a resource for you to come back to throughout the design process.

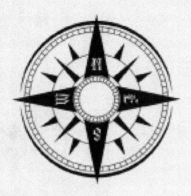

NAVIGATING THE WATERS: MINI-GAMES, ALTERNATIVE ASSESSMENTS, AND SIDE QUESTS

The idea is to fill every expedition with some adventure and small, unexpected challenges that add a thrilling experience to the journey. You need to have layers of challenges that create epic moments within your game.

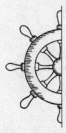

You need to have layers of challenges that create epic moments within your game.

SETTING THE COURSE

Pick a route and answer the question(s). Then move to the next section, "Exploring," and further define the details. Start with the route that excites you the most and then come back to the others later.

ROUTE ONE: STORY

What mini-games or fillers do you think would fit best into the story you created? Think of ways to wrap these into your storyline and theme.

ROUTE TWO: STUDENT CHOICE

Side quests allow students to choose their own adventure. What type of quest will you design as a choice for your students?

ROUTE THREE: ASSESSMENT

How can you move beyond the bubble of standard assessments in your classroom? Where and when can you shake up your assessments?

EXPLORE PHASE

Now that you have chosen a route, it is time to craft the details. Use the general ideas you created above, and spend time exploring possible names, characteristics, and connections. If you get stuck or lose motivation, move on to a new route and come back later with fresh eyes.

EXPLORE ROUTE ONE: STORY

- The first five minutes of class: think of a quick way to start your class off with energy and excitement.
- Last five minutes of class: How can you end class with a bang and make your students excited for the next class?
- Are the mini-games you chose driven by your content or simply a fun break from the curriculum? Is there a way to connect different reviews together with games?
- Think of titles that connect the mini-games, assessments, and side quests to your theme.

EXPLORE ROUTE TWO: STUDENT CHOICE

- Are you going to offer your students choices from a list of different side quests? Do more side quests become available as the game progresses?
- Can students create their own side quests? For example, students can create the rubrics and decide how they fit into the larger game. You can also have students complete side quests created by other students.
- Will you link side quests to grades or will they earn separate XP?
- What opportunities are there within your game for students to control what happens in the game?
- How could you add an element of Status, Access, or Power to student choice?

Explore Route Three: Assessment

- Do all students have to complete the same assessments? Could they be limited to only students with certain badges?
- What kind of alternative assessments could you build using a game mechanic? For example, in a Boss Battle, the group could decide who is strong enough to take an "alternate" test.
- What kinds of powers could an item or badge have on an assessment? (e.g., Staff of Wisdom: 50/50 on a multiple choice question)

Where could you fit an alternative assessment into your class? (e.g., test review, group challenge on the actual assessment)

Dropping Anchor

If the highest aim of a captain
were to preserve his ship,
he would keep it in port forever.

—*Thomas Aquinas*

You have done it! You have sailed the vast seas of gamification and begun the process of dedicated, playful planning to amplify your course content and motivate your students to engage at even greater depths of learning. Now it is time to drop anchor and set foot in the New World, the place where your visions for game-based learning come to life. This book is your fully equipped ship, with its sails, cargo, and lessons learned from the newly explored routes; it will help you build an engaged settlement filled with lifelong explorers in the New World of education.

Believe in your plan to launch this method of teaching and harness the creative winds that filled your sails while you navigated this book. Surround yourself with fellow buccaneers who will support you as you venture into this new territory. Many like us around the world are building upon one another's new discoveries and treasured examples

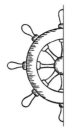 **Believe in your plan to launch this method of teaching and harness the creative winds that filled your sails while you navigated this book.**

of student achievement. We must combine our passionate energies and new resources in order for this way of teaching and learning to take hold and revolutionize the fossilized ways of education that no longer serve our students.

Spread the word with me that building game-inspired courses also helps us build self-actualized, confident, lifelong learners. Games connect people; they inspire us to do the impossible by working together to reach our fullest potential. Game-based learning provides opportunities to take risks, to fail, and to try again with newly acquired knowledge of the content and ourselves.

Early on, students will notice your approach has changed, and they will be actively curious. Trust builds when you show them your excitement and invite them to explore this new way of learning with you. The members of your diverse crew of learners will surprise themselves and one another with different emotions, expectations, and skills to tackle the content within the new framework. This is to be celebrated! They will rely on one another in new ways, applaud classmates and fellow players for reaching new heights, and offer sympathy when disappointments crash them against the rocks. School will suddenly become as engaging as the adventures they seek beyond its walls. Ready your-self for learners who will request more of these opportunities to define their talents, their passions, and their desires to leave legacies. And then brace yourself, matey, for the thrill it will ignite in you as you follow the call to imagine, design, and grow within a content-filled and experience-rich classroom in the New World. Now, what will your story be?

School will suddenly become as engaging as the adventures they seek beyond its walls.

Compass Rose

More from

DAVE BURGESS
Consulting, Inc.

Teach Like a PIRATE

Increase Student Engagement, Boost Your Creativity, and Transform Your Life as an Educator

By Dave Burgess (@BurgessDave)

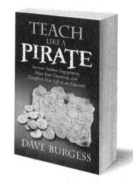

Teach Like a PIRATE is the *New York Times*' best-selling book that has sparked a worldwide educational revolution. It is part inspirational manifesto, that ignites passion for the profession, and part practical road map, filled with dynamic strategies to dramatically increase student engagement. Translated into multiple languages, its message resonates with educators who want to design outrageously creative lessons and transform school into a life-changing experience for students.

P is for PIRATE
Inspirational ABC's for Educators
By Dave and Shelley Burgess
(@Burgess_Shelley)

Teaching is an adventure that stretches the imagination and calls for creativity every day! In *P is for Pirate*, husband and wife team Dave and Shelley Burgess encourage and inspire educators to make their classrooms fun and exciting places to learn. Tapping into years of personal experience and drawing on the insights of more than seventy educators, the authors offer a wealth of ideas for making learning and teaching more fulfilling than ever before.

Ditch That Textbook
Free Your Teaching and
Revolutionize Your Classroom
By Matt Miller (@jmattmiller)

Textbooks are symbols of centuries-old education. They're often outdated as soon as they hit students' desks. Acting "by the textbook" implies compliance and a lack of creativity. It's time to ditch those textbooks—and those textbook assumptions about learning! In *Ditch That Textbook*, teacher and blogger Matt Miller encourages educators to throw out meaningless, pedestrian teaching and learning practices. He empowers them to evolve and improve on old, standard teaching methods. *Ditch That Textbook* is a support system, toolbox, and manifesto to help educators free their teaching and revolutionize their classrooms.

Learn Like a PIRATE
Empower Your Students to
Collaborate, Lead, and Succeed
By Paul Solarz (@PaulSolarz)

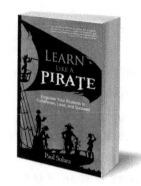

Today's job market demands that students be prepared to take responsibility for their lives and careers. We do them a disservice if we teach them how to earn passing grades without equipping them to take charge of their education. In *Learn Like a Pirate*, Paul Solarz explains how to design classroom experiences that encourage students to take risks and explore their passions in a stimulating, motivating, and supportive environment where improvement—rather than grades—is the focus. Discover how student-led classrooms help students thrive and develop into self-directed, confident citizens who are capable of making smart, responsible decisions, all on their own.

Pure Genius
Building a Culture of Innovation and
Taking 20% Time to the Next Level
By Don Wettrick (@DonWettrick)

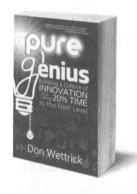

For far too long, schools have been bastions of boredom, killers of creativity, and way too comfortable with compliance and conformity. In *Pure Genius*, Don Wettrick explains how collaboration—with experts, students, and other educators—can help you create interesting, and even life-changing, opportunities for learning. Wettrick's book inspires and equips educators with a systematic blueprint for teaching innovation in any school.

50 Things You Can Do with Google Classroom
By Alice Keeler and Libbi Miller

It can be challenging to add new technology to the classroom, but it's a must if students are going to be well-equipped for the future. Alice Keeler and Libbi Miller shorten the learning curve by providing a thorough overview of the Google Classroom App. Part of Google Apps for Education (GAFE), Google Classroom was specifically designed to help teachers save time by streamlining the process of going digital. Complete with screenshots, *50 Things You Can Do with Google Classroom* provides ideas and step-by-step instructions to help teachers implement this powerful tool.

Master the Media
How Teaching Media Literacy Can Save Our Plugged-in World
By Julie Smith

Written to help teachers and parents educate the next generation, *Master the Media* explains the history, purpose, and messages behind the media. The point isn't to get kids to unplug; it's to help them make informed choices, understand the difference between truth and lies, and discern perception from reality. Critical thinking leads to smarter decisions—and it's why media literacy can save the world.

The Zen Teacher
Creating Focus, Simplicity, and Tranquility in the Classroom
By Dan Tricarico

Teachers have incredible power to influence, even improve, the future. In *The Zen Teacher,* educator, blogger, and speaker Dan Tricarico provides practical, easy-to-use techniques to help teachers be their best—unrushed and fully focused—so they can maximize their performance and improve their quality of life. In this introductory guide, Dan Tricarico explains what it means to develop a Zen practice—something that has nothing to do with religion and everything to do with your ability to thrive in the classroom.

The Innovator's Mindset
Empower Learning, Unleash Talent, and Lead a Culture of Creativity
By George Couros

The traditional system of education requires students to hold their questions and compliantly stick to the scheduled curriculum. But our job as educators is to provide new and better opportunities for our students. It's time to recognize that compliance doesn't foster innovation, encourage critical thinking, or inspire creativity—and those are the skills our students need to succeed. In *The Innovator's Mindset,* George Couros encourages teachers and administrators to empower their learners to wonder, to explore—and to become forward-thinking leaders.

Bring the *eXPlore like a Pirate* message to your school!

Want to be a game-changer in education? Then eXPlore the creative and engaging waters of game-inspired course design with Michael Matera at your next event!

Michael will equip your participants with practical skills in gamification—whether you're looking for an all-day, idea-packed workshop, a motivational keynote about the New World of education, or a single, topic-specific conference session.

Michael Matera's Most Popular Keynotes Include:

- Playful Planning: What Games Can Teach Us About Learning
- Push Play: Beginning Gamification in Your Classroom
- Beyond the Badge: Mechanics to Build up Your Gamification Toolbox
- Mini-Games: Unlocking the Potential of Play

Host a Plugin Play Workshop

Plugin Play is all about functionality and ease. This workshop builds your plugin play gamification model. Working through the core components of theme, points, badges, and game mechanics, you will leave with a blueprint for success. Additionally, you will learn how to use the game-inspired design process to construct your own rich experience for your students. Come ready to learn and earn your way through this workshop, as you will be unlocking your ideas and your students' potential.

Learn more @ ExploreLikeAPirate.com/speaking

About the Author

Michael Matera has taught for more than a decade, using interactive play, passion, and purpose-driven learning to transform the classroom in international, public, and private schools. He is a pioneer in the field of education, using gamification and technology to increase authentic student engagement and content acquisition. Along with being a full-time teacher at University School of Milwaukee, Michael is also a nationally-known presenter and international consultant of game-based learning. He was named one of ASCD's Emerging Leaders in 2015 for infusing best practices in the field with accessible, gamified teaching methods. He is also an educational Bam! Radio talk-show host and blogger, whose mission is to build connections among innovative, global educators. Michael is driven to transform education through theoretical and technological applications that identify and inspire limitless learning thresholds in educators and students. Join the transformation of education by visiting ExploreLikeAPirate.com, co-founded educational blog, edbean.com, and on Twitter @mrmatera.

CPSIA information can be obtained
at www.ICGtesting.com
Printed in the USA
FSHW021908160519